From the Kitchen of

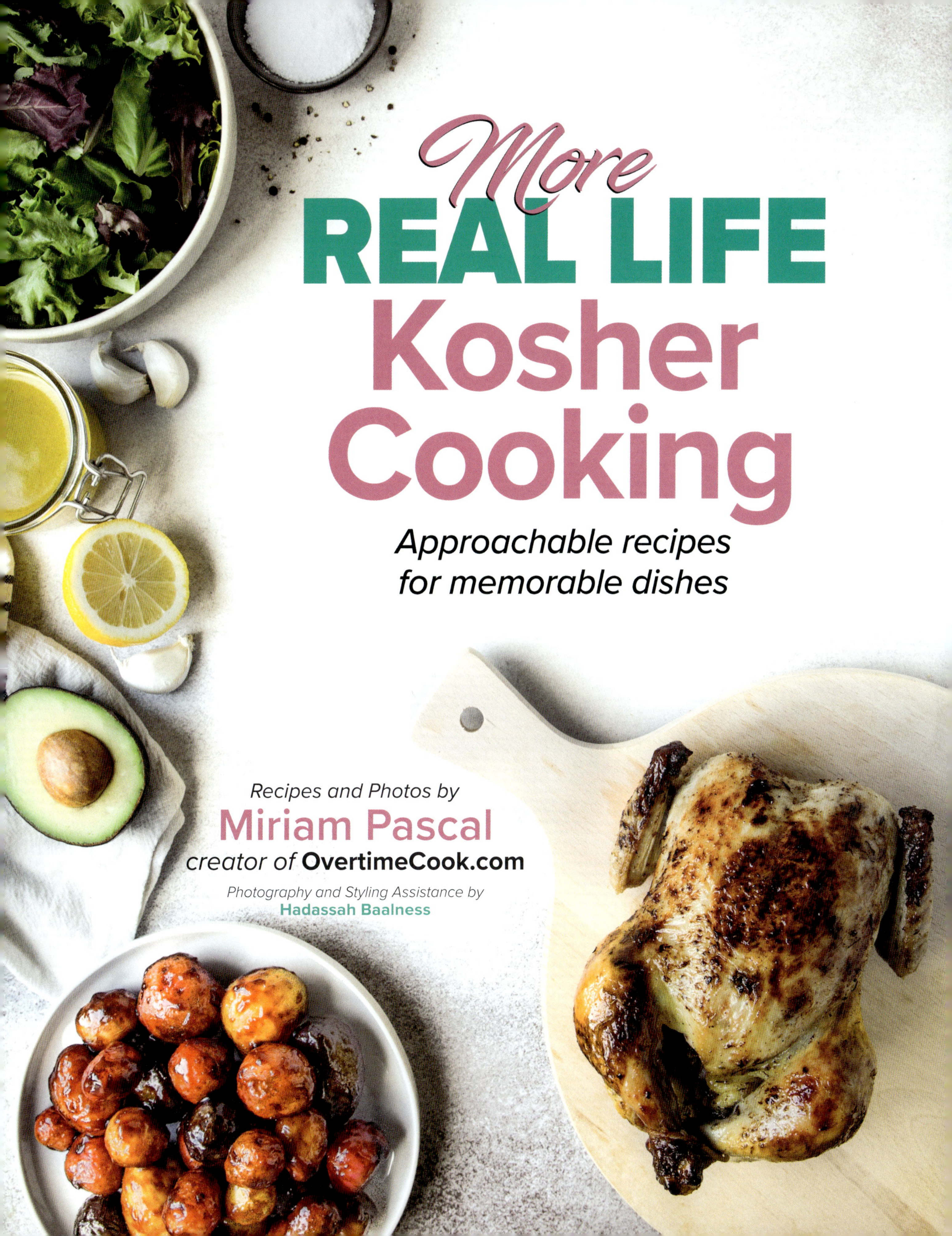

More REAL LIFE Kosher Cooking

Approachable recipes for memorable dishes

Recipes and Photos by
Miriam Pascal
creator of **OvertimeCook.com**

Photography and Styling Assistance by
Hadassah Baalness

First Edition — First Impression / November 2019

Published by **ARTSCROLL / SHAAR PRESS**
4401 Second Avenue / Brooklyn, NY 11232 / (718) 921-9000 / www.artscroll.com

Distributed in Israel by **SIFRIATI / A. GITLER**
POB 2351 / Bnei Brak 51122 / Israel

Distributed in Europe by **LEHMANNS**
Unit E, Viking Business Park, Rolling Mill Road
Jarrow, Tyne and Wear / NE32 3DP, England

Distributed in Australia and New Zealand by **GOLDS WORLD OF JUDAICA**
3-13 William Street / Balaclava, Melbourne 3183, Victoria / Australia

Distributed in South Africa by **KOLLEL BOOKSHOP**
Northfield Centre, 17 Northfield Avenue
Glenhazel 2192 / Johannesburg, South Africa

ISBN-10: 1-4226-2531-1 / ISBN-13: 978-1-4226-2531-6

Printed in Canada

Acknowledgments

THANK YOU TO...

My life has often led me down twists and turns that ultimately were indeed pushes in the direction that I needed to go to get where I am today. For that, I thank **HASHEM**, Who has given me the strength, talent, and ability to pull this off, and Who guided me here.

When people ask where I learned to cook, I always say that it was natural for me, growing up with two creative and adventurous cooks for parents. Thank you to my wonderful parents, **HARRY AND NECHAMA PASCAL**, for helping me become the cook — and the person — that I am today.

Where would I be without my amazing family? They are my taste-testers, my cheering squad, my helpers, and my inspiration. Thank you to **YAAKOV AND FREIDI PASCAL**, **CHAYA AND YONI KRAMER**, **SARAH AND EZRA MASSRY**, **MORDY AND CHEVY PASCAL**, and **LEAH AND EPHRAIM NUSSBAUM** for being the best siblings I could ever ask for. Thank you to my nieces and nephews for being my most honest and adorable tasters: **CHAYALA**, **MIRI**, **MIRIAM**, **TOVA**, **ALIZA**, **SARA**, **CHAYALA**, **YAAKOV**, **NESANEL**, **MORDECHAI**, **AVI**, **SHAUL**, and **RIVKY**!

I can't single out the **FRIENDS** who have been my invaluable support system as I spent the last two years working on this book, whether it was looking over my table of contents to make sure there was a good variety in the book, helping me troubleshoot a problem recipe, shlepping me out of the house when I clearly needed a break, or simply being a listening ear and a supportive friend. Thanks to all of you — you know who you are!

I would not have made it through intense weeks of photoshoots for this book without my incredible **KITCHEN STAFF**, who patiently and expertly created the food you see on these pages. Thank you so much to **SARI ELLER**, **BLIMA SILVERSTEIN**, and **AVA ZUCKER**!

Thank you to **RIVKY KLEIMAN** and **YUSSIE WEISZ** for sharing their recipes with me.

Thank you to my talented and patient photography and styling assistant, **HADASSAH BAALNESS**, for helping me create beautiful images to showcase the food in this book!

Thank you to **CHANIE NAYMAN** and the whole team at **MISHPACHA MAGAZINE** for allowing me to share my recipes with your readers and for being the inspiration for some of the recipes in this book.

Thank you to **RABBI GEDALIAH ZLOTOWITZ** for believing in me and my books, and for giving me another opportunity to share my recipes with the world.

When someone's job is to correct you, it's often hard to like them. But with my incredible editor, **FELICE EISNER**, that's not the case. Thank you for your patience, for your skill, and for making me a better writer.

Thank you to the proofreaders, **TOVA OVITS** and **JUDI DICK**, for your helpful suggestions. Thank you to **BRUCHA BILLER** for proofreading everything I write, but especially this book. Thank you to **SHAINDY SHMAYE** for your proofreading assistance.

Thank you to **ELI KROEN** for your beautiful cover design, as always. Thank you to **RIVKA WEISS** for all of your hard work and talents that you put into making this book beautiful and clear. Thank you to **DEVORAH COHEN** for designing the original layout. Thank you to **MIREL GOLDWASSER** for your design advice and expertise.

As always, the last (and certainly not least) thank-you goes to my loyal **FANS AND FOLLOWERS**. Every photo you send makes my day. Every comment you write spurs me on. Every question you ask teaches me something. This book has been written because of your feedback and support, so thank you!

Thank You to My Recipe Testers

Thank you to MIRIAM ROSENTHAL for your hard work and organization coordinating all of the recipe testing.

Chani Aaron ■ Natalie Adelman ■ Rivka Adelman ■ Hadassah Baalness ■ Nechama Bachrach ■ Sue Barash ■ Lauren Beer ■ Devorah Beida ■ Steffi Berke ■ Lauryn Berman ■ Brucha Biller ■ Esther M. Braun ■ Kayla Brown Yhakubovich ■ Chaya Bruk ■ Rachel Bryks ■ Zack Burack ■ Chaya Sara Ceitlin ■ Ortal Cohen ■ Chanie Davidsohn ■ Michelle Dolgin ■ Shevy Dubin ■ Elisheva Ettlinger ■ Yael Fogel ■ Leora Freishtat ■ Esty Fried ■ Shifra Gerber ■ Jennifer Gertelman ■ Aviva Gluck ■ Adina Goldberg ■ Shana Goldman ■ Shaina Gordon ■ Leyna Goro ■ Shulamith Grauman ■ Elisa Gurevich ■ Arielle Haft ■ Nati Har-Sinay ■ Chani Herman ■ Sara Hojda ■ Debra Inger ■ Vicki Isakow ■ Arielle Jacobowitz ■ Rachel Jacobs ■ Rochelle Jacobs ■ Donna Karp ■ Alice Katchen ■ Aviva Katz ■ Elisheva Katz ■ Chaya Kramer ■ Dena Krinsky ■ Tovah Landa ■ Chana Lapine ■ Estee Lavitt ■ Carol Lazar ■ Rivka Lazar ■ Shani Lehrer ■ Daphna Levine ■ Rebecca Linzer ■ Miriam Lipnick ■ Genendy Loeb ■ Shoshana Markowitz ■ Tamar May ■ Michele Meiner ■ Rivky Mitteldorf ■ Devorah Nussbaum ■ Karen Ohayon ■ Atara Paris ■ Freidi Pascal ■ Alumah Pitterman ■ Liora Posin Afrah ■ Shifra Poznanski ■ Tzippi Robinson ■ Rebecca Rose ■ Naomi Rosenman ■ Hillary Rosenthal ■ Kathy Rosillo ■ Leala Rosner ■ Jessica Roth ■ Shira Rudski ■ Hadassah Sanker ■ Jessica Saunders ■ Baila Schloss ■ Amelia Schmidt ■ Penina Schoenfeld ■ Robyn Schwager ■ Aliza Schwartz ■ Amy Schwartz ■ Sori Schwartz ■ Avigayil Sheinfeld ■ Adina Shyovitz ■ Chavi Simpson ■ Lavinia Solganik ■ Talia Stansbury ■ Moshe Statman ■ Stephanie Steinbock ■ Estee Stern ■ Esti Stern ■ Shifra Stitzer ■ Meryl Strauss ■ Lisa Strimber ■ Angela Vaisman ■ Rebecca Vegh ■ Helen Weg ■ Shaina Weiss ■ Baila Werczberger ■ Cindy Wiesel ■ Chavi Zeitz

Table of Contents

Dairy and Meatless Mains

Vegetables and Sides

Desserts and Drinks

Baked Goods and Pastries

Sauces and Staples

Introduction

As a (now) three-time cookbook author, I often receive emails and messages from aspiring food writers, asking for advice about writing a cookbook of their own. And my response to them is always the same: Why?

Why do you want to write a cookbook? A cookbook shouldn't be written "just because." It shouldn't be written to check an item off on an accomplishments checklist. You need to have a good reason.

So why did I write this cookbook? It's simple, really: I had to.

It started in November 2017, when my second cookbook, ***Real Life Kosher Cooking***, came out. Within less than a week, every single recipe in the book appeared in my inbox, in the form of a photo, a glowing review, or both. The feedback from all over the world was incredible. It was overwhelming. And I knew that as hard as it was, and as much work as it entailed, I had to do it all over again. I was privileged enough to change people's lives through the food — my food — they were cooking, and that, in turn, changed my life. I don't think that the people who have sent feedback on my recipes over the 8½ years that I've been sharing them will ever fully understand the impact they've made by sharing their feedback, their photos, their comments, and yes, even their critiques. They have all spurred me on, encouraged me, forced me to keep going.

I believe that, first and foremost, food has to taste good. But through the taste (and sometimes aroma or feel) of food, we create memories. And those memories are as important as the taste itself. Good food is about the love that goes into it, and the experiences you have while enjoying it. When I look at the recipes and photos that grace the pages of this book, I don't just think about the incredible tastes and delicious smells that accompany them. I think about the memories that are associated with each dish.

I look at the photo of the **Moroccan Cauliflower Soup** and I remember that rainy cold day that I spent with my sisters. We went to a cafe for lunch and ordered a similar soup. It was so comforting and perfect, I knew I'd go home and recreate it. When I think about my **Sweet and Spicy Pretzels** recipe, I remember the Purim that I included a package of them in my shalach manos. I remember getting texts all day from friends and family asking, "What was in those pretzels? I can't stop eating them!" When I look at the **Cornmeal Waffles**, I'm transported to a lazy Sunday brunch in my home. I've invited my sisters, sisters-in-law and their kids, and we're enjoying waffles. Grownups top theirs with the Maple Blueberry Sauce; the kids top theirs with whipped cream and tons of sprinkles. Everyone is happy and content.

The **Braised Beef with Tortellini** recipe brings me back to the first day of Succos. I've invited my entire family to share a meal in the succah. It's one of the first chilly days that fall, and everyone smiles when I bring out steaming bowls of this comforting stew as the appetizer. The recipe for the **Slow-Roasted Garlic and Jalapeño Dip** always makes me think of my brother's favorite contribution to any Shabbos meal, and the **Spice-Rubbed Chicken Thighs** remind me of my picky-eater niece, who said it's her favorite chicken recipe in the entire world.

Just a glance at the photo of the **Overnight Onions** makes me smile because I can close my eyes and smell Friday morning in my mother's kitchen, when these came out of their overnight oven stay and smelled so good you couldn't help tasting some, even though it's early in the morning. And my recipe for **Tropical Blue Punch** will forever be associated with girls' night in, sharing good cocktails and good conversation with my friends until the early hours of the morning. **Peanut Butter Crinkle Cookies** remind me of the first time I made them. A few of my nieces and nephews were over, and they wanted to bake. I found the ingredients in my pantry and the kids all took turns "helping" me pour in the sugar, eggs, and other ingredients.

Creamy Pea Soup will always be associated with my contribution to a potluck family dinner at my sister's house. **Eggplant and Japanese Yam Salad** will forever remind me of a fun lunch with friends. **Sticky Blueberry Chicken** will always be about my father raving to me about "that amazing chicken you made that time." And the **Wontons in Garlic Sauce** recipe will always make me smile because I know how excited my family will be when I serve it at a festive meal. It's their favorite recipe in this book, after all.

Food has the power to be transformative. I've always striven for recipes that are approachable and doable. Recipes that will make you say, "I can do that!" Recipes that will get you in the kitchen, making food, but more importantly, making memories. Because my goal, through writing this book, is that you should go through the (hopefully stained and marked-up) pages of your own copy, and remember a whole new set of memories that you've created with your loved ones.

And that is why I've written this book. Because sharing my recipes, helping you to create delicious food and special moments, is my passion in life. It gives me enormous joy, and I can't stop.

Here's to good food, and good memories.

Miriam

overtimecook.com | overtimecook@gmail.com

Recipe Notes

- All recipes use kosher salt, unless specified otherwise. Other salts, such as table salt, have varied levels of saltiness, and are therefore not spoon-for-spoon replacements.
- Use a neutral oil such as canola oil, unless specified otherwise.
- Flour is all-purpose flour, unless specified otherwise.
- Lemon and lime juice in all recipes is freshly squeezed. Using bottled juice may result in a different or less intense flavor.
- Recipes were tested using metal baking pans, not disposable. Due to lower heat conduction, disposable pans generally require longer cooking time and yield less crispy results.

CAULIFLOWER RICE SHAKSHUKA, PAGE 18

CORNMEAL WAFFLES WITH MAPLE BLUEBERRY SAUCE PAGE 12

SOFT PRETZELS, PAGE 28

GRANOLA MUFFINS, PAGE 16

HEALTHY LEMON CHEESE PANCAKES, PAGE 14

HOMEMADE PITA, PAGE 26

Breakfast *and* Breads

Cornmeal Waffles
with Maple Blueberry Sauce

Dairy or Pareve | Yield 8 servings

These summer-inspired waffles are going to wow your brunch guests with flavors and textures reminiscent of blueberry corn muffins, all in an attractive waffle dish!

WAFFLES

1½ cups flour

1¼ cups cornmeal

⅓ cup sugar

1 Tablespoon baking powder

½ teaspoon sea salt

1 teaspoon vanilla extract

1½ cups milk OR nondairy milk

3 eggs

½ cup oil

MAPLE BLUEBERRY SAUCE

4 cups blueberries, fresh or frozen

¼ cup pure maple syrup

¼ cup sugar

1 teaspoon cinnamon

¼ cup lemon juice

1 Tablespoon cornstarch dissolved in **2 Tablespoons** cold water

whipped cream OR vanilla ice cream, optional, for serving

1. **Prepare the waffles:** In a medium bowl, whisk together flour, cornmeal, sugar, baking powder, and salt. Whisk to combine. Add remaining waffle ingredients; stir until a smooth batter forms.
2. Cook according to your waffle maker instructions; set aside.
3. **Meanwhile, prepare the maple blueberry sauce:** In a small pot, combine blueberries, maple syrup, sugar, cinnamon, and lemon juice in a small pot. Bring to a boil over high heat; reduce heat and simmer for 10 minutes. Add cornstarch and water mixture (slurry); cook for 1-2 minutes, until thickened.
4. Serve warm sauce over waffles. Top with whipped cream or ice cream, if desired.

Plan Ahead Waffles can be prepared ahead and frozen, well wrapped. Reheat in the oven, uncovered, on a cookie sheet, until warmed through. Maple Blueberry Sauce will stay fresh in the fridge for up to 1 week.

Healthy Lemon Cheese Pancakes

Dairy | Yield 6 servings

These pancakes are bright and fresh, easy to make, and — oh! did I mention — they're packed with protein and on the healthy side. A winner breakfast if I ever saw one!

1 (16-ounce) container low fat cottage cheese

2 (6-ounce) containers plain Greek yogurt

4 eggs

2 cups white whole wheat flour, divided

½ cup honey

¼ cup sugar OR sweetener

1 teaspoon vanilla extract

1 teaspoon baking powder

½ teaspoon baking soda

½ cup milk

zest and juice of **2** lemons

¼ teaspoon lemon extract, optional but recommended

oil or nonstick cooking spray, for frying

pure maple syrup OR honey, optional, for serving

1. In the bowl of a blender, combine cottage cheese, yogurt, eggs, 1 cup flour, honey, sugar, vanilla, baking powder, baking soda, milk, lemon zest, lemon juice, and lemon extract, if using. Blend until smooth. Add remaining 1 cup flour; blend again until completely smooth.
2. Heat a small amount of oil in a large, nonstick frying pan. Pour scoops of batter, about ⅓ cup each, into pan.
3. Fry over medium heat for about 3 minutes, until bubbles form on the top. Flip; fry for about 1 more minute. Remove pancakes from pan; repeat with remaining batter.
4. Serve with maple syrup, if desired.

Variations For additional flavor and texture, before flipping pancakes, top with blueberries or chocolate chips.

Plan Ahead Batter can be prepared ahead and refrigerated for up to 2 days. Fry fresh, just before serving.

Granola Muffins

Dairy or Pareve | Yield 16 muffins

Granola lovers, here's your new favorite on-the-go breakfast. These whole wheat muffins are topped with that delicious crunch of granola .... I won't judge if you eat them all day, instead of saving them just for breakfast!

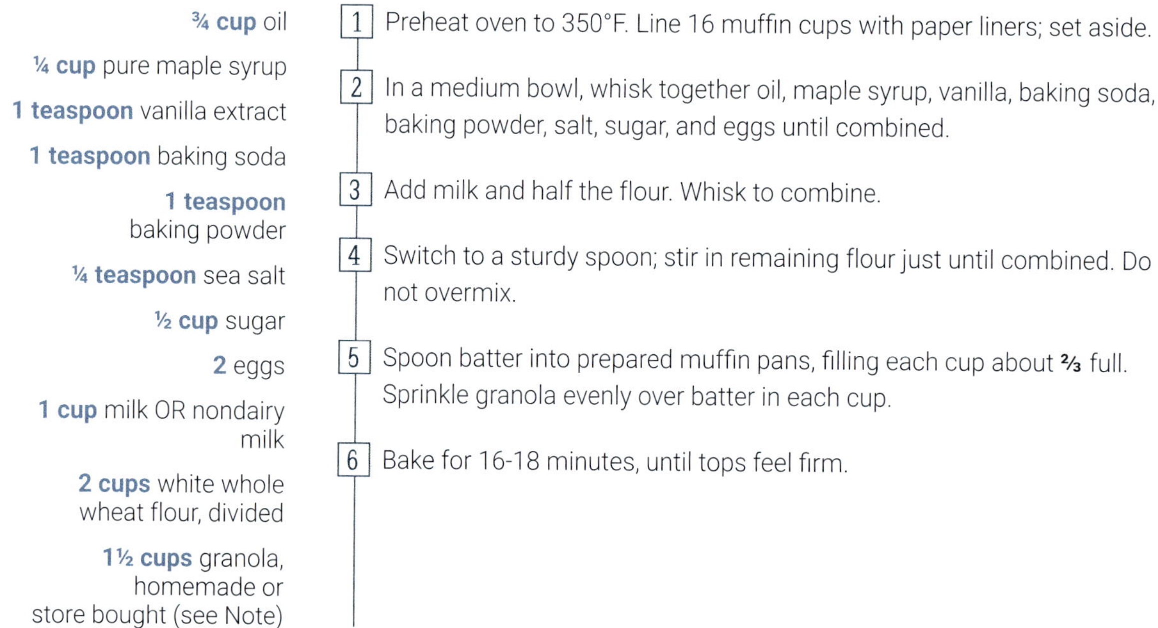

- **¾ cup** oil
- **¼ cup** pure maple syrup
- **1 teaspoon** vanilla extract
- **1 teaspoon** baking soda
- **1 teaspoon** baking powder
- **¼ teaspoon** sea salt
- **½ cup** sugar
- **2** eggs
- **1 cup** milk OR nondairy milk
- **2 cups** white whole wheat flour, divided
- **1½ cups** granola, homemade or store bought (see Note)

1. Preheat oven to 350°F. Line 16 muffin cups with paper liners; set aside.
2. In a medium bowl, whisk together oil, maple syrup, vanilla, baking soda, baking powder, salt, sugar, and eggs until combined.
3. Add milk and half the flour. Whisk to combine.
4. Switch to a sturdy spoon; stir in remaining flour just until combined. Do not overmix.
5. Spoon batter into prepared muffin pans, filling each cup about ⅔ full. Sprinkle granola evenly over batter in each cup.
6. Bake for 16-18 minutes, until tops feel firm.

Note You can use the granola you like best in this recipe. If you don't want to make your own, pick up a bag at the grocery store. If you have homemade granola, definitely use it! ■ Here's a quick recap of the Easy Homemade Granola from my book, *Real Life Kosher Cooking*: Toss ½ cup each rolled oats, slivered almonds, chopped pecans, sunflower seeds, and raisins or cranberries with ¼ cup each oil, honey, and brown sugar, with 1 teaspoon each cinnamon and vanilla extract and a pinch of kosher salt. Spread on a parchment paper-lined baking sheet; bake at 350°F for 20-30 minutes. Let cool, then break into clusters.

Plan Ahead These muffins freeze well in an airtight container or bag.

Cauliflower Rice Shakshuka

Pareve | Yield 3-4 servings

One of my favorite ways to cook a really filling breakfast is to make a shakshuka that's loaded with veggies. I've played around with various combinations, but none are more satisfying than this cauliflower rice version. As a bonus, it's filling on its own — even without bread — so it's great for a diet-friendly or low-carb breakfast, too!

1 Tablespoon olive oil
1 large onion, finely diced
3 cloves garlic, minced
2 teaspoons kosher salt
1 (12-ounce) bag frozen cauliflower rice
1½ teaspoons cumin
1 teaspoon sugar, optional
1 teaspoon turmeric
1 teaspoon smoked paprika
1 teaspoon chili powder
2 teaspoons red wine vinegar
1 (6-ounce) can tomato paste
1 (28-ounce) can tomato purée
1 cup water
6-8 eggs
kosher salt, to taste
black pepper, to taste

1. Heat oil in a large, deep frying pan over medium heat. Add onion, garlic, and salt. Sauté for 5 minutes, stirring occasionally, until softened.
2. Add cauliflower rice, cumin, sugar, turmeric, smoked paprika, chili powder, and vinegar. Stir and cook for 5-8 minutes.
3. Add tomato paste, tomato purée, and water. Cover pan and bring mixture to a boil; reduce heat and simmer for 5 minutes.
4. Working with 1 egg at a time, crack the egg into a small bowl. Make a well in the veggie mixture and slip the egg into it. Repeat with remaining eggs. Sprinkle salt and pepper over each egg. Cover shakshuka; cook over medium-low heat, until the eggs are cooked to your desired level of doneness (about 8 minutes for a runny yolk).

Plan Ahead Cauliflower rice mixture can be made a day or two ahead. Reheat sauce before adding eggs. Eggs should be cooked in the sauce just before serving.

Broccoli and Cheddar Frittata

Dairy | Yield 4-6 servings

Broccoli and cheddar cheese are such a classic and delicious pairing, I decided to combine them into this delicious frittata — a perfect, no-bake option for your next brunch!

2 Tablespoons oil

1 Spanish onion, diced

2 teaspoons kosher salt, divided

1 pound frozen broccoli, defrosted and drained

3 cloves garlic, minced

10 eggs

½ cup milk (preferably full fat)

½ teaspoon black pepper

¾ cup shredded cheddar cheese

1. Heat oil in a large, deep frying pan over medium heat. Add onions and 1 teaspoon salt; cook about 5 minutes, until softened.
2. Squeeze as much liquid out of the broccoli as you can. Chop broccoli into bite-size pieces; add to pan. Add garlic. Cook for 10 minutes, stirring occasionally.
3. Meanwhile, in a large bowl, whisk together eggs, milk, remaining teaspoon salt, and pepper until smooth. Add cooked vegetables; stir to combine.
4. Grease pan (no need to wash it out first) and return it to stove over high heat. Pour egg and vegetable mixture into pan. Sprinkle cheese over the top.
5. Turn heat to medium-low; cover pan tightly. Cook for about 15 minutes, until cooked through and slightly puffy.

Plan Ahead Vegetables can be sautéed a day or two ahead and stored in the fridge. Frittata should be prepared just before serving.

Puff Pastry Breakfast Pizza

Dairy | Yield 8 mini pizzas

While I was growing up, breakfast and brunch on special occasions were lengthy affairs, with my father standing at the stove, making a custom egg order for each person using his famous cast-iron pan. He always enjoyed making food for the family, but we always felt a little guilty that we'd inevitably be finished eating before he got a chance to sit down and enjoy his own egg. Pondering this problem, I came up with this breakfast-for-a-crowd solution that's not only a crowd pleaser, but nobody has to be a short order cook!

SAUCE

1 cup tomato sauce

3 cloves garlic, minced

2 cubes frozen basil

PIZZAS

8 large (5-inch) puff pastry squares

2 Tablespoons dried minced onions

1½ cups shredded mozzarella cheese

8 eggs

kosher salt, to taste

black pepper, to taste

1. Preheat oven to 400°F. Line a baking sheet with parchment paper; set aside.
2. **Prepare the sauce:** In a small bowl, combine tomato sauce, garlic, and basil. Set aside.
3. **Prepare the pizzas:** Fold over ¼-inch of the edges of each puff pastry square, to form a tiny crust. Place on prepared baking sheet. Top each square with tomato sauce mixture; sprinkle minced onions over the surface.
4. Place shredded cheese around the inside edge of each square, leaving an indentation in the center. Working with one egg at a time, crack an egg into a small bowl. Slip the egg inside a circle of cheese. Sprinkle salt and pepper over egg. Repeat with remaining eggs and squares.
5. Bake for 18-20 minutes, until the top of the egg is set.

Plan Ahead This dish is best enjoyed fresh.

Quick and Easy Whole Wheat Sandwich Bread

Pareve | Yield 1 Loaf

When I wondered which bread recipes to include in this book, I thought about what I find myself buying most often, and my mind immediately went to whole wheat sandwich bread — a staple in my house. You'll be pleasantly surprised at how easy it is to make it yourself — and, of course, it's so much better than anything you'll buy!

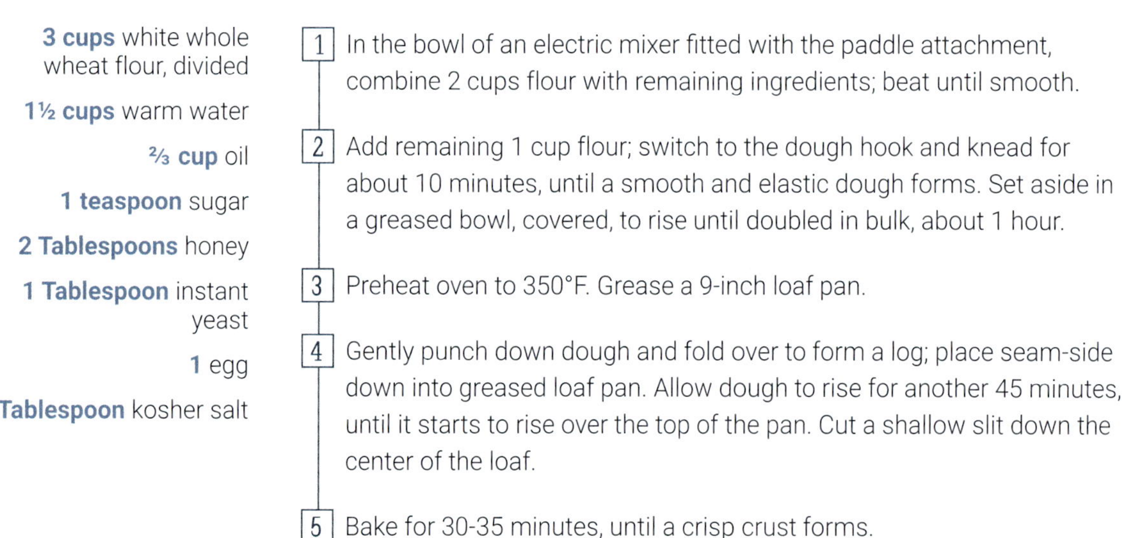

3 cups white whole wheat flour, divided

1½ cups warm water

⅔ cup oil

1 teaspoon sugar

2 Tablespoons honey

1 Tablespoon instant yeast

1 egg

1 Tablespoon kosher salt

1. In the bowl of an electric mixer fitted with the paddle attachment, combine 2 cups flour with remaining ingredients; beat until smooth.
2. Add remaining 1 cup flour; switch to the dough hook and knead for about 10 minutes, until a smooth and elastic dough forms. Set aside in a greased bowl, covered, to rise until doubled in bulk, about 1 hour.
3. Preheat oven to 350°F. Grease a 9-inch loaf pan.
4. Gently punch down dough and fold over to form a log; place seam-side down into greased loaf pan. Allow dough to rise for another 45 minutes, until it starts to rise over the top of the pan. Cut a shallow slit down the center of the loaf.
5. Bake for 30-35 minutes, until a crisp crust forms.

Plan Ahead Bread can be frozen, wrapped well, until ready for use.

Homemade Pita

Pareve | Yield 8 pitas

There's something exhilarating about watching homemade pitas come together. Partly because they're so incredibly easy, but mostly because it's almost magical to put disks of dough into the oven and pull out puffy pillows of delightful bread 4 minutes later!

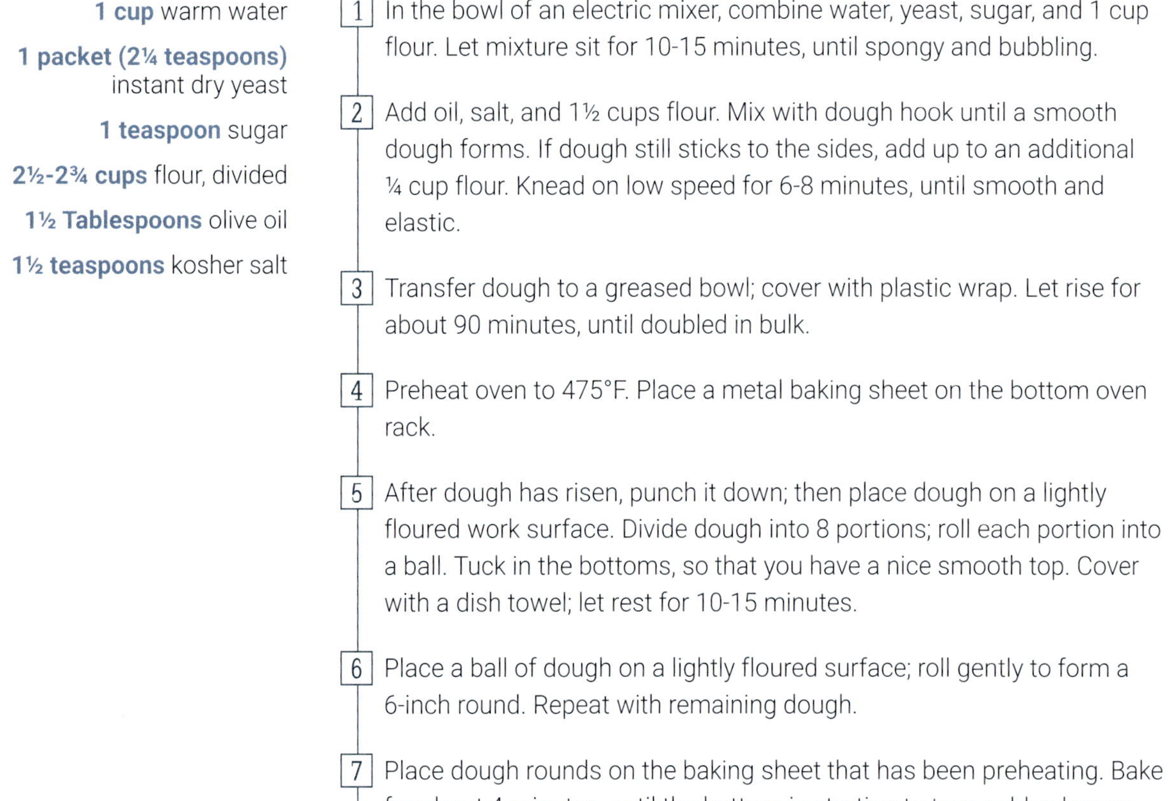

1 cup warm water

1 packet (2¼ teaspoons) instant dry yeast

1 teaspoon sugar

2½-2¾ cups flour, divided

1½ Tablespoons olive oil

1½ teaspoons kosher salt

1. In the bowl of an electric mixer, combine water, yeast, sugar, and 1 cup flour. Let mixture sit for 10-15 minutes, until spongy and bubbling.
2. Add oil, salt, and 1½ cups flour. Mix with dough hook until a smooth dough forms. If dough still sticks to the sides, add up to an additional ¼ cup flour. Knead on low speed for 6-8 minutes, until smooth and elastic.
3. Transfer dough to a greased bowl; cover with plastic wrap. Let rise for about 90 minutes, until doubled in bulk.
4. Preheat oven to 475°F. Place a metal baking sheet on the bottom oven rack.
5. After dough has risen, punch it down; then place dough on a lightly floured work surface. Divide dough into 8 portions; roll each portion into a ball. Tuck in the bottoms, so that you have a nice smooth top. Cover with a dish towel; let rest for 10-15 minutes.
6. Place a ball of dough on a lightly floured surface; roll gently to form a 6-inch round. Repeat with remaining dough.
7. Place dough rounds on the baking sheet that has been preheating. Bake for about 4 minutes, until the bottom is starting to turn golden brown. Pitas will be puffy, but will deflate as they cool. Remove to a plate; cover the plate with a kitchen towel. The towel will retain the heat generated by the steam and it will keep the pitas soft.

Plan Ahead While there's nothing quite like bread fresh from the oven, these pitas can be frozen, well wrapped, until ready to serve.

Soft Pretzels

Pareve | Yield 10 large pretzels

Soft pretzels are a food that's full of nostalgia for me. When I was growing up, my mother would buy the frozen kind and we'd melt cheese on top for a really delicious treat. When I got older and was introduced for the first time to fresh, homemade soft pretzels, I was astonished. How could something that I already enjoyed so much be this much better?

DOUGH

1¼ cups warm water
1 packet (2¼ teaspoons) instant dry yeast
2 Tablespoons sugar
2 teaspoons kosher salt
2 Tablespoons oil
4 cups flour

FOR BOILING

12 cups water
¾ cup baking soda

FOR TOPPING

1 egg yolk
1 teaspoon water
coarse pretzel salt

1. **Prepare the dough:** Combine water, yeast, and sugar in the bowl of an electric mixer fitted with the dough hook. Let sit for a few minutes, until foamy.
2. With the mixer on low speed, add salt, oil, and flour. Mix until a dough is formed.
3. Increase mixer speed; knead for 6-8 minutes, until dough is smooth and elastic. Place dough into a greased bowl, cover, and let rise in a warm place for about 1 hour, until doubled in bulk.
4. Preheat oven to 450°F. Line 2 baking sheets with parchment paper; set aside.
5. Divide dough into 10 equal portions. Roll 1 portion into a long, thin rope, about 20 inches long. Bring the edges of the rope up, cross them over each other, cross them a second time, then fold down over the center to form the pretzel shape. Place on prepared baking sheet. Repeat with remaining dough.
6. **Boil the pretzels:** Bring water and baking soda to a rolling boil in a large pot. Working in batches so as not to overcrowd the pot, slip 2-3 pretzels into the water; boil for 45 seconds. Carefully remove pretzels (it's easiest to do this with a flat spatula); return to baking sheet. Repeat with remaining pretzels.
7. **Prepare the topping:** Combine egg yolk and water in a small bowl. Brush mixture over each pretzel, then sprinkle with coarse salt.
8. Bake for about 13 minutes, until golden brown.

Plan Ahead Soft pretzels are best fresh from the oven, but they can be prepared and frozen until ready to serve. Reheat, uncovered, until warmed through.

HUMMUS AND MUSHROOM PLATTER, PAGE 50

SALSA CHICKEN TOSTADAS PAGE 42

APRICOT-LIME-GLAZED CHICKEN WINGS, PAGE 34

WONTONS IN GARLIC SAUCE, PAGE 32

PASTA CHIP NACHOS, PAGE 54

SPICY COCOA ROASTED NUTS, PAGE 58
SWEET AND SPICY PRETZELS, PAGE 58

Appetizers *and* Snacks

Wontons in Garlic Sauce

Meat | Yield 10-12 servings

This recipe began with my obsession with wontons and garlic sauce from a particular Chinese restaurant that's nowhere near my home. Naturally, I had to recreate it myself. Since then, these wontons have become the stuff of Pascal family legend. It's my family's all-time favorite Yom Tov appetizer. The only downside? It's pretty much guaranteed to upstage basically any other dish you serve at the same meal!

WONTONS

1½ pounds ground beef

2 Tablespoons soy sauce

½ teaspoon toasted sesame oil

2 Tablespoons sesame seeds, preferably a mix of black and white

4 scallions, sliced

4 cloves garlic, minced

50 wonton wrappers, approximately

GARLIC SAUCE

1 (18-ounce) jar hoisin sauce

⅓ cup soy sauce

⅓ cup rice vinegar

⅓ cup honey

2 teaspoons sriracha

1 teaspoon ground mustard

½ teaspoon ground ginger

½ cup water

12 cloves garlic, minced

sliced scallions, optional, for garnish

additional sesame seeds, optional, for garnish

1. **Prepare the wontons:** Combine beef, soy sauce, sesame oil, sesame seeds, scallions, and garlic in a large bowl; stir gently until just combined.

2. Place about 2 teaspoons meat mixture onto the center of a wonton wrapper. Brush a small amount of water along the edges before pressing them together to help keep them sealed; bring the edges together to form a wonton. Set aside; repeat with remaining meat and wonton wrappers.

3. Bring a pot of salted water to a boil. Drop a few wontons into the boiling water; cook for about 6 minutes, until the meat is cooked through. Work in batches to avoid overcrowding the pot. Remove wontons with a slotted spoon; place on parchment paper, not touching each other. Set wontons aside.

4. **Meanwhile, prepare the garlic sauce:** Combine all sauce ingredients in a medium pot. Bring to a boil, then reduce heat; simmer mixture for about 15 minutes, stirring occasionally, until sauce thickens.

5. Just before serving, toss cooked wontons in sauce; warm through. If desired, garnish with sliced scallions and sesame seeds.

Plan Ahead Wontons can be frozen, without sauce, either before cooking (boil just before serving; if boiling frozen, add 1 minute to cooking time) or after cooking. Sauce can be prepared up to 3 days ahead and stored in the fridge. Combine wontons and reheated sauce just before serving.

Apricot-Lime-Glazed Chicken Wings

Meat | Yield 4-6 servings

Did you know that there's a scientific reason that some people are able to tolerate heat in their food more than others? That's right – it's something to do with the taste receptors in your mouth. Here's a little secret for you: I'm one of those people whose mouth simply can't handle the heat! And because wings are almost always served with a spicy sauce, my quest for the perfect wings sauce started. I didn't want anything too sweet, so I came up with this sweet and tangy sauce. Together with crispy wings, it creates an incredibly satisfying appetizer!

WINGS

2 pounds chicken wings, separated into drumettes and flats (see Note)

1 Tablespoon oil

1 teaspoon kosher salt

½ teaspoon black pepper

2 Tablespoons cornstarch

APRICOT-LIME SAUCE

¾ cup apricot jam

2 Tablespoons soy sauce

2 cloves garlic, minced OR 2 cubes frozen garlic

1 teaspoon kosher salt

juice of 2 limes

1. **Prepare the wings:** Toss wings with oil, salt, and pepper. Add cornstarch; toss until cornstarch has dissolved.

2. **Oven Method:** Preheat oven to 450°F. Line a baking sheet with parchment paper; place wings on baking sheet. Bake for about 30 minutes, flipping halfway through, until chicken is cooked through.

   Air Fryer Method: Preheat air fryer to 375°F. Place wings into fry basket; cook for 12 minutes. Flip wings; cook for 12 minutes. Raise air fryer temperature to 400°F; cook for 6 minutes.

3. **Meanwhile, prepare apricot-lime sauce:** Combine all sauce ingredients in a small pot. Whisk until smooth. Bring mixture to a boil over high heat, then reduce heat to low; simmer for 5 minutes.

4. To serve, toss wings together with sauce.

Note Wings are easier to eat and they cook more evenly when they're split into the drumette (the part that look like a miniature drumstick) and the flat, which consists of parallel flat bones. (The tip is generally not sold with kosher chicken wings.) If your meat market doesn't sell them separately, ask the butcher to split them, or do it yourself by cutting through the joint.

Plan Ahead Sauce can be made up to a week ahead and stored in the fridge. Wings are best fresh, but if necessary, they can be prepared a day or two ahead and reheated in the oven, in a single layer, until warmed through.

Pull-Apart Appetizer Pie

Meat | Yield 2 pies, 6 servings each

This is one of my most popular and requested appetizer recipes. It's pretty on the platter, fun to eat, and an ultimate crowd-pleaser with kids and grownups alike. The quantities and measurements here are more of a guide than an exact recipe, so feel free to adjust the ingredients to suit your taste or what you have on hand.

- **10-12 large (5-inch)** puff pastry squares
- **4-5** hot dogs
- **6-8 ounces** sliced deli, such as pastrami and/or corned beef
- **1 cup** mashed potatoes (see Note)
- **2 Tablespoons** spicy brown mustard
- **2 Tablespoons** duck sauce
- additional duck sauce, optional, for serving
- Honey Mustad Dressing (page 66), optional, for serving

1. Preheat oven to 350°F. Grease 2 (8-inch) round pans; set aside.
2. **Prepare the hot dog rolls:** Wrap a piece of puff pastry around a hot dog; press to seal. Repeat with remaining hot dogs.
3. **Prepare the deli rolls:** Place deli slices on a puff pastry square, alternating between meats. Roll up pinwheel style. Repeat with remaining deli.
4. **Prepare the potato rolls:** Place ⅓ of the mashed potatoes in a strip across the center of a puff pastry square. Roll the pastry up around it to form a log shape. Repeat with remaining mashed potatoes.
5. Cut each rolled pastry into 5-6 equal parts. Arrange the pieces in prepared baking pans, touching but not tightly packed. The appetizers will grow into each other and stick together as they bake.
6. Combine mustard and duck sauce in a small bowl; brush generously onto pastry.
7. Bake for 50-60 minutes, until tops are golden brown.
8. To serve, slip out onto a serving platter. Serve with duck sauce or Honey Mustard Dressing.

Note I'm not generally a fan of instant mashed potatoes, but they work well here and save time. I add crispy fried onions (such as French's) to the potatoes. They lose their crispness but add delicious flavor and texture.

Variation Include only those fillings you like, or add others, such as spiced ground beef, pulled beef, or other favorite. You can also bake them in a rectangular pan or prepare them freeform on a baking sheet, as shown.

Plan Ahead This recipe can be frozen until ready to serve. You can freeze it raw and bake it when needed, or freeze it fully baked. If freezing it baked, reheat, uncovered, until warmed through.

Sweet and Sticky Grilled Sausages

Meat | Yield 4-6 servings

Do you ever have those moments where you have a bunch of guests coming, and at the last minute you panic, thinking that you won't have enough food? Yeah, me too. And that's how this recipe was born. In one such situation, I raided my fridge and found the ingredients for this dish – an instant family favorite! (Turns out, I totally had enough food, even without these, but hey, they were finished to the last bite anyway!)

1 (16-ounce) package kielbasa

¼ cup duck sauce

¼ cup chili sauce (I use Heinz)

1 Tablespoon soy sauce

1 Tablespoon apple cider vinegar

1 Tablespoon honey

1 teaspoon garlic powder

1. Slice kielbasa on a bias (diagonally); place into a large bowl. Add remaining ingredients; toss until sausage slices are fully coated. Marinate mixture in the fridge for 20-30 minutes.
2. Preheat oven to broil. Line a baking sheet with foil.
3. Spread sausage slices in a single layer on prepared baking sheet. Broil on high for 6-8 minutes, flipping halfway through, until just starting to char.

Plan Ahead These sausages are great straight from the broiler, but can be reheated the next day, for a Shabbos meal, for example. Heat, loosely covered, until warmed through.

Meat-Stuffed Garlic Bread

Meat | Yield 8 servings

Everyone loves garlic bread, but when you hide a meat surprise in the center, it becomes an instant sensation. One of my favorite things about this appetizer is how well it freezes — so make a big batch and keep it on hand for those times when you want to serve something really special.

GARLIC PESTO

1 cup garlic cloves

¼ cup fresh parsley

½ cup olive oil

1½ teaspoons kosher salt

MEAT FILLING

1 Tablespoon oil

1 pound ground beef OR veal

ASSEMBLY

24 mini (2-3 inch) pizza dough rounds

1 egg

1. Preheat oven to 400°F. Line a baking sheet with parchment paper; set aside.
2. **Prepare the garlic pesto:** Place all pesto ingredients into a blender jar. Blend until mixture is completely smooth. You can also do this using an immersion blender and placing ingredients into a tall container. Set aside.
3. **Prepare the meat filling:** Heat oil in a large frying pan over high heat. Add meat; cook, stirring to break up the lumps, for a few minutes, until meat starts to brown. Add about ½ cup of garlic pesto; stir well to combine.
4. **Assemble the garlic bread:** In a small bowl, whisk together about ¼ cup garlic pesto and egg. Set aside for topping.
5. Brush a layer of garlic pesto over 1 pizza dough round. Top with about 1 tablespoon meat mixture, then fold dough around filling. Stretch the dough as you work to make sure it will enclose the filling. Place filled round, seam-side down, on prepared baking sheet. Repeat with remaining dough and filling. Reserve remaining pesto.
6. Brush reserved pesto and egg mixture generously over the top of each filled round. Bake for 20 minutes, or until golden brown.

Plan Ahead Meat-stuffed garlic bread can be prepared ahead and frozen until ready to serve. Rewarm, uncovered, until heated through.

Salsa Chicken Tostadas

Meat | Yield 8 servings

One of the great signs of a successful recipe, in my opinion, is the percentage of people who taste it and then ask (even beg!) for the recipe. The good news is, this recipe is batting 1000 – so far, everyone who's tasted these tostadas has requested the recipe! For a fun and interactive way to serve it, do it deconstructed style: Place all the elements into bowls and let your guests assemble their own.

CRISPY TORTILLAS

8 (6-inch) corn tortillas

kosher salt, for sprinkling

SALSA CHICKEN

2 teaspoons oil

4 baby (dark) chicken cutlets

1 (16-ounce) jar salsa of your choice

ASSEMBLY

Guacamole (page 288), or store-bought

Pico de Gallo, optional (page 288)

1. **Prepare the crispy tortillas:** Preheat oven to 400°F. Line 2 baking sheets with parchment paper; set aside.
2. Cut each tortilla into quarters. Spray both sides of each piece well with nonstick cooking spray. Sprinkle with salt. Place tortillas in a single layer (do not overlap) on prepared baking sheets.
3. Bake for 8-10 minutes, flipping halfway through, until crispy. Set aside to cool.
4. **Prepare the salsa chicken:** Heat oil in a frying pan over high heat. Add chicken; sear for about 2 minutes per side, until browned. Chicken will still be raw on the inside. Remove from pan and set chicken aside until it's cool enough to handle. Cut into very small pieces, then return to the pan over medium heat.
5. Add salsa; cook, stirring occasionally, for about 5 minutes, until chicken is cooked through.
6. **Assemble the salsa chicken tostadas:** Place salsa chicken on a crispy tortilla chip. Top with Guacamole and Pico de Gallo, if using.

Plan Ahead Crispy tortillas can be prepared a few days ahead and stored in an airtight bag, or frozen until ready for use. Chicken can be prepared up to two days ahead and kept refrigerated. Assemble and rewarm, covered, until heated through.

Braised Beef with Tortellini

Meat | Yield 8 appetizer servings

I'll always think of this as a Succos dish, because that's when this dish made its debut. It was a cool day in the succah, and bringing out steaming bowls of fall-apart soft meat served with delicious pasta was the perfect appetizer to set the tone for the holiday meal.

MEAT

- 2 Tablespoons oil , plus more for searing
- 2 pounds beef chuck stew meat, cut in bite-size chunks
- kosher salt, for sprinkling
- black pepper, for sprinkling
- 3 medium Spanish onions, diced
- 2 teaspoons kosher salt, divided
- 1 head celery, diced
- 3 large carrots, peeled and diced
- 4 cloves garlic, minced
- 1½ cups red wine (preferably semi-dry)
- ½ cup pomegranate juice (see Note)
- 1 cup orange juice
- 2 Tablespoons honey
- ¼ teaspoon black pepper
- 1 teaspoon dried sage
- 1 teaspoon dried thyme
- 1 teaspoon ground ginger
- about 1 cup vegetable broth OR water
- 1 (12-ounce) package tomato tortellini, prepared according to package directions

1. To sear beef, heat a thin layer of oil in a large pot over high heat.
2. Sprinkle salt and pepper over the meat, then add to the pot. Working in batches to prevent overcrowding the pan, sear beef chunks for 1-2 minutes per side, until browned; remove from pan and set aside.
3. Heat remaining 2 tablespoons oil over medium heat in the same pot. Add onions and 1 teaspoon salt. Cook for about 5 minutes, until softened.
4. Add celery, carrots, and garlic. Cook for about 10 minutes, until vegetables are softened and fragrant.
5. Add wine, pomegranate juice, orange juice, honey, remaining teaspoon salt, pepper, sage, thyme, and ginger.
6. Add seared beef cubes to pot. Stir to combine; add up to a cup of broth or water to cover.
7. Cover pot; bring to a boil. Reduce heat; simmer for 3-4 hours, until meat is fork-tender.
8. Just before serving, stir in the cooked tortellini.

Note If you don't have pomegranate juice, use an additional ½ cup wine instead. You can also replace the tortellini with any small pasta.

Variation You can prepare the meat in a crockpot instead of on the stovetop. Prepare recipe through Step 6, then transfer to a crockpot and cook for about 6 hours, until meat is soft.

Plan Ahead Meat and its sauce can be prepared ahead and frozen until ready to serve. Reheat, covered, over gentle heat, until warmed through. Add cooked pasta just before serving.

Duo of Stuffed Mushrooms

Meat or Pareve | Yield each recipe yields 2 dozen stuffed mushrooms

These delicious stuffed mushrooms are my go-to appetizer for those special meals when I want something on the healthy side, without feeling that it's too dietetic.

Meat-Stuffed Mushrooms

MUSHROOMS

2 dozen large white mushrooms, stems removed

olive oil, for drizzling

kosher salt, for drizzling

black pepper, for drizzling

MEAT/MUSHROOM STUFFING

1 pound ground beef

¾ cup fresh parsley, chopped

5 cloves garlic, minced

1 Tablespoon Dijon mustard

zest of 1 lemon

juice of 1 lemon

1 teaspoon kosher salt

1. Preheat oven to 450°F. Line a baking sheet with parchment paper; set aside.
2. **Prepare the stuffing:** In a large bowl, combine all stuffing ingredients,
mixing gently to combine.
3. Drizzle olive oil, salt, and pepper into the cavities of each mushroom cap.
4. **Prepare the mushroom caps:** Place mushrooms on prepared pan; bake for 10 minutes. Fill each cavity with meat mixture, heaping it over the top. Bake about 10 minutes until mushrooms are crispy on bottom and the meat is cooked through.

Note Any extra vegetable stuffing can be placed on the baking sheet to bake alongside the mushrooms; serve as a side or simply nosh on it after the pan comes out of the oven.

Plan Ahead Both types of stuffed mushrooms can be refrigerated for a day or two and rewarmed, uncovered, until warmed through.

Vegetable-Stuffed Mushrooms

MUSHROOMS

2 dozen large white mushrooms, stems reserved

olive oil, for drizzling

kosher salt, for drizzling

black pepper, for drizzling

VEGETABLE STUFFING

2 Tablespoons olive oil

1 onion, finely diced

2 teaspoons kosher salt, divided

reserved mushroom stems, finely chopped

4 cloves garlic, minced

1 orange bell pepper, finely diced

1 red bell pepper, finely diced

1 yellow bell pepper, finely diced

1 Tablespoon red wine vinegar

1 teaspoon dried oregano

1 teaspoon hot sauce

1 egg, lightly beaten

⅓ cup breadcrumbs

1. **Prepare the stuffing:** Heat oil in a large frying pan over medium heat. Add onion and 1 teaspoon salt; sauté for 5 minutes, until softened.
2. Add mushroom stems, garlic, peppers, vinegar, oregano, remaining teaspoon salt, and hot sauce. Cook over medium low heat for 20-30 minutes, until vegetables are softened and fragrant.
3. **Meanwhile, prepare the mushroom caps:** Preheat oven to 450°F. Line a baking sheet with parchment paper.
4. Place mushroom caps on baking sheet. Drizzle with olive oil, salt, and pepper. Bake for 10 minutes.
5. Remove stuffing mixture from heat; stir in egg and breadcrumbs. Stuff mixture into parbaked mushroom caps, piling them high over the edge. Return to oven; bake about 20 minutes, until mushrooms are golden brown.

Crispy Onion Strings

With Tangy Maple Aioli

Pareve | Yield 4-6 servings

This recipe is in honor of a good friend of mine, Chana Miriam, who shares my love of crispy onion rings and always shares an order of them with me when we go out together. Here's my crispy homemade version: Using strings instead of rings means it's easier to make, and loads of fun to eat! Eat them as is, as a snack, add them to a salad for a great crunch, or place some on top of steak as a great garnish.

2 eggs

1 teaspoon kosher salt

1 teaspoon garlic powder

1 teaspoon paprika, preferably smoked

2 teaspoons sugar

1 cup cornstarch

1 Tablespoon rice vinegar

2 large Spanish onions, thinly sliced

oil, for frying

TANGY MAPLE AIOLI

½ cup mayonnaise

1 Tablespoon spicy brown mustard

2 Tablespoons pure maple syrup

1 Tablespoon apple cider vinegar

kosher salt, to taste

1 teaspoon sriracha OR hot sauce

1. In a large bowl, whisk together eggs, salt, garlic powder, paprika, and sugar until smooth.
2. Add cornstarch and rice vinegar; whisk to form a stiff batter. Add up to 1 tablespoon water if the batter is too thick. Add onions; toss until fully coated.
3. Heat about an inch and a half of oil in a large, deep frying pan over medium-high heat. Add a few onion slices at a time, stirring to prevent them from forming into clumps. The fewer you add at one time, the less likely they are to clump (see Variation). Fry for about 3 minutes, stirring occasionally, until golden brown and crispy. Remove to paper towel to drain. Work in batches to avoid overcrowding the pan, stirring to recoat onions in batter before adding each batch to the oil.
4. **Prepare the tangy maple aioli:** Combine all aioli ingredients in a small bowl; whisk to combine. Serve as a dipping sauce for Crispy Onion Strings.

Plan Ahead Crispy Onion Strings are best enjoyed fresh, but you can refrigerate them and then reheat a day or two later if necessary. Reheat in a single layer, uncovered, until warmed through.

Variation To make onion latkes, don't separate the onion strings when you place them in the oil. They will clump up and fry together to form delicious latkes.

Hummus and Mushroom Platter

Pareve | Yield 8-10 servings

There are some dishes that I'll always order when I see them on a restaurant menu; Hummus with Mushrooms is one of them. I love the contrast of the creamy hummus, the slow-cooked mushrooms, and all of these wonderful flavors! Feel free to make just the hummus for a delicious homemade version of this popular dip.

HUMMUS

- 2 (15.5-ounce) cans chickpeas
- juice of 2 lemons
- 4 cloves garlic
- ½ cup tahini paste
- ¼ cup olive oil
- ⅓ cup ice water
- 1½ teaspoons kosher salt
- 1½ teaspoons cumin

MUSHROOMS

- ¼ cup olive oil
- 12-14 ounces white mushrooms, diced
- 12-14 ounces baby bella mushrooms, diced
- 4 cloves garlic, minced
- 1½ teaspoons kosher salt
- ½ teaspoon black pepper
- ¼ cup fresh chopped parsley OR 2 teaspoons dried parsley
- 1 teaspoon cumin
- 1 Tablespoon balsamic vinegar
- olive oil, for garnish
- fresh parsley, for garnish

1. **Prepare the hummus:** Reserve ⅓ cup liquid from the canned chickpeas. Discard remaining liquid; rinse and drain chickpeas.
2. Place chickpeas into the bowl of a food processor fitted with the "S" blade. Pulse a few times to coarsely chop the chickpeas.
3. Add reserved chickpea liquid and remaining ingredients. Process for a few minutes until combined and very creamy.
4. **Prepare the mushrooms:** Heat oil in a large frying pan over medium heat. Add mushrooms and garlic. Cook, stirring occasionally, for 25-30 minutes, until browned and reduced in size.
5. Add salt, pepper, parsley, cumin, and balsamic vinegar. Raise heat to high; cook, stirring frequently, for 5-6 minutes until mixture has darkened and liquid has been absorbed.
6. **To assemble:** Spread hummus on a platter, making an indentation in the center. Place mushrooms into the indentation. Drizzle with olive oil and parsley.

Plan Ahead Hummus can be made 2-3 days ahead and stored in the fridge. Mushroom mixture can be made 2-3 days ahead and stored separately in the fridge. For best results, assemble platter just before serving.

Salmon Avocado Spring Rolls

Pareve | Yield 12 spring rolls

I originally made these together with my friend Miriam R. at her house. As they came out of the pan, her kids Shani, Shuly, and Shaindy hovered around, excitedly tasting and exclaiming how much they liked it. When a recipe gets two thumbs-up from the grownups AND the kids, I know it's a winner!

- **½ cup** sweet chili sauce
- **1 Tablespoon** soy sauce
- juice of **1** lime
- **3** salmon fillets
- **12** spring roll wrappers
- **1** avocado, very thinly sliced
- oil OR nonstick cooking spray
- sweet chili sauce, optional, for serving

1. Preheat oven to 350°F.
2. Place sweet chili sauce, soy sauce, and lime juice into a small bowl; stir to combine.
3. Place salmon into a baking pan into which they fit snugly. Pour a generous amount of sauce over each fillet. Reserve any remaining sauce.
4. Bake for 20 minutes, if frying in Step 7; or 16 minutes if air frying or baking in Step 7. Remove and discard salmon skin; flake fish into large pieces with a fork; return to pan.Add reserved sauce; stir to distribute evenly.
5. **Assemble the spring rolls:** Place a spring roll wrapper diagonally. Overlap 2-3 slices avocado in the center, so the avocado slices fill about 4 inches of the wrapper. Top with 2-3 tablespoons salmon flakes.
6. Fold the sides of the spring roll over the salmon and avocado, then fold over the top. Roll toward the bottom, as tightly as possible. Wet your finger in a cup of water, then use your finger to wet the tip of the wrapper and press to seal. Repeat with remaining ingredients.
7. **Frying method:** Heat about 1½ inches oil over medium heat in a deep frying pan or pot. Fry spring rolls, a few at a time for about 1 minute, then flip and fry for an additional 30-45 seconds, until golden brown. Drain on paper towels. Serve with sweet chili sauce, optional.

   Air fryer method: Spray both sides of each spring roll well with nonstick cooking spray, then place a few into the basket of air fryer. Cook at 375°F for 5 minutes, then flip and cook at 400°F for 3 minutes until crispy. Serve with sweet chili sauce, optional

   Oven method: Preheat oven to 450°F. Spray both sides of each spring roll well with nonstick cooking spray. Place on a parchment-lined baking sheet; bake for 8 minutes, until crispy. Serve with sweet chili sauce, optional.

Notes Instead of serving with sweet chili sauce, double the sauce mixture and use as a dip for the spring rolls. ■ The baked salmon with the sauce is delicious on its own, as well.

Plan Ahead Spring rolls can be prepared a day or two ahead. Refrigerate, then rewarm, uncovered, until heated through.

Pasta Chip Nachos

Dairy | Yield 6 Servings

I have very mixed feelings about nachos. While I enjoy them, I'm always the one to protest ordering them in a restaurant. My issue? Within minutes of arriving at the table, the nachos are inevitably soggy. Every time. My solution? Pasta chip nachos. These ridiculously crispy chips aren't just tastier and more fun to eat than the traditional kind. They're harder, and therefore they stay crunchy (believe it or not!) all the way until the plate is licked clean!

PASTA CHIPS

1 (1-pound) box lasagna noodles

oil, for frying

kosher salt, for sprinkling

CHEESE SAUCE

½ stick (4 Tablespoons) butter

¼ cup flour

1 teaspoon kosher salt

1 teaspoon ground mustard

½ teaspoon black pepper

1½ cup whole milk, divided

8 ounces shredded cheddar cheese

FOR SERVING

Pico de Gallo (page 288) OR store-bought salsa

1 avocado, diced

1. **Prepare the pasta chips:** Boil lasagna noodles to "al dente" according to package directions. Cool, then cut noodles into triangles.
2. Heat about 1½ inches oil in a large, deep frying pan. Working in batches to avoid overcrowding the pan, add several pasta triangles; fry for 2-3 minutes per side, until golden brown and crispy. Drain on paper towels; immediately sprinkle with kosher salt. Set aside.
3. **Prepare the cheese sauce:** Melt butter in a large pot over medium heat. Add flour; whisk until smooth. Cook for 1-2 minutes, whisking often, until the mixture starts to brown.
4. Add salt, mustard, and pepper. Whisk to combine.
5. Add half the milk; whisk to incorporate. Continue to cook for 2-3 minutes, until the mixture starts to thicken.
6. Add cheese; cook, stirring often, for about 5 minutes, until cheese is melted and mixture is smooth. Add remaining milk; stir until incorporated and totally smooth.
7. **Assemble the nachos:** Place chips on a large platter. Drizzle with cheese sauce; top with Pico de Gallo, avocado, and other toppings, if desired (see Note).

Note You can add your favorite nachos toppings to this dish, such as sour cream, corn, black beans, sliced olives, and pickled hot peppers.

Plan Ahead Chips can be prepared ahead and stored for up to a week in an airtight bag. Cheese sauce can be prepared a day or two ahead. Rewarm over low heat, stirring often, until softened. Add additional milk, as necessary, to bring it back to the correct texture.

Falafel-Coated Chickpeas

Pareve | Yield about 2 cups

For years, I've been making falafel-spiced chickpeas, adding them to salads or noshing on them for a boost of protein. One day, I was staring at a package of falafel ball mix, and it hit me ... why spice my chickpeas like falafels when I can coat them in it?

1 Tablespoon olive oil

2 Tablespoons tahini paste

1½ teaspoons kosher salt

1 teaspoon cumin

1 (15.5-ounce) can chickpeas, drained and rinsed

1 pouch (6 Tablespoons) falafel mix

1. Preheat oven to 425°F. Line a baking sheet with parchment paper; set aside.
2. In a medium bowl, whisk together oil, tahini, salt, and cumin. Add chickpeas; toss to coat. Add dry falafel mix; toss until all chickpeas are coated.
3. Spread coated chickpeas on prepared baking sheet. Bake for 20 minutes, until crispy.

BBQ Roasted Corn Kernels

Pareve | Yield 2 cups

These delicious tidbits are great as a snack, and they work really well as a fun side dish as well. They're reminiscent of popcorn, yet somehow more filling!

1 (16-ounce) bag frozen corn kernels

1 Tablespoon canola oil

½ teaspoon kosher salt

½ (heaping) teaspoon garlic powder

½ (heaping) teaspoon onion powder

½ (heaping) teaspoon paprika (preferably smoked)

¼ teaspoon black pepper

1. Preheat oven to 400°F. Line a baking sheet with parchment paper.
2. In a large mixing bowl, combine all ingredients.
3. Spread on prepared baking sheet.
4. Bake for about 30 minutes, until starting to turn brown and crispy.

Plan Ahead Falafel-Coated Chickpeas can be prepared a day or two ahead. For best results, reheat, uncovered, to re-crisp.

Plan Ahead BBQ Corn Kernels can be prepared a day or two ahead and enjoyed at room temperature.

Spicy Cocoa Roasted Nuts

Pareve | Yield 2½ cups

These nuts are a symphony of flavors — sweet, salty, and bitter — coming together to make an incredible snack that will have you and your family going back for more!

3 Tablespoons oil

2 Tablespoons honey

1 Tablespoon cocoa powder

1½ teaspoons cinnamon

1 teaspoon kosher salt

¼ teaspoon ground ginger

¼ teaspoon cayenne pepper

2½ cups raw nuts of your choice

1. Preheat oven to 400°F. Line a baking sheet with parchment paper; set aside.
2. In a large bowl, whisk together first 7 ingredients until a smooth, thick paste forms. Add nuts; toss well to fully coat.
3. Spread nuts on prepared baking sheet. Depending on the size of the nuts, bake for 12-15 minutes, stirring halfway through. Set aside to cool completely, then store in an airtight container until ready to serve.

Plan Ahead Nuts will stay fresh for about 1 week when stored at room temperature in an airtight bag or container.

Sweet and Spicy Pretzels

Pareve | Yield 6-8 servings

I made these incredibly tasty snacks for my shalach manos last year, and all Purim I received texts from friends and family saying, "What were those pretzel things? I can't stop eating them!" After one taste, you'll understand why everyone was desperate for the recipe.

1 teaspoon kosher salt

1 teaspoon smoked paprika

1 teaspoon cumin

1 teaspoon chili powder

1 teaspoon cinnamon

⅛ teaspoon cayenne pepper

⅓ cup dark brown sugar

1 cup oil

1 (12-ounce) bag salted pretzels

1. Preheat oven to 200°F. Line a baking sheet with parchment paper; set aside.
2. In a large bowl, whisk together spices, sugar, and oil until smooth. Add pretzels; toss until evenly coated.
3. Transfer pretzels to prepared baking sheet. Bake for 1 hour, stirring halfway through baking time.
4. Set aside to cool before serving.

Plan Ahead Pretzels can be prepared up to a week ahead and stored in an airtight bag or container.

THE ORIGINAL LIGHT PILSNER

GRILLED CHICKEN AND BROCCOLI SALAD WITH ROASTED TOMATO VINAIGRETTE, PAGE 64

SNAP PEA, CORN, AND CABBAGE SALAD, PAGE 72

STEAK AND PEPPER SALAD WITH LEMON DRESSING, PAGE 62

RAINBOW SALAD, PAGE 76

ASIAN BROCCOLI AND QUINOA SALAD, PAGE 82

THANKSGIVING SALAD, PAGE 68

Salads *and* Spreads

Steak and Pepper Salad
with Lemon-Dill Dressing

Meat | Yield 6-8 servings

I often think of this as "the Shabbos lunch salad," because it's one of my favorite recipes that's a guaranteed crowd-pleaser with just enough of a "wow" factor. For a lighter version, use grilled chicken instead of steak.

1 (approx. 2-pound) London broil

LEMON-DILL DRESSING/MARINADE

¾ cup fresh dill, chopped

4 cloves garlic, minced

juice of **2** lemons

1 teaspoon kosher salt

⅓ cup olive oil

1½ Tablespoons honey

PEPPER MIXTURE

2 Tablespoons oil

1 small onion, sliced

4 cloves garlic, minced

1½ teaspoons kosher salt

1 red bell pepper, sliced into strips

1 orange or yellow bell pepper, sliced into strips

SALAD

12 ounces romaine lettuce

1½ cups snow peas, halved

1 avocado, sliced or diced

1. **Prepare the lemon-dill dressing/marinade:** Place all dressing ingredients into a small bowl. Whisk to combine.

2. **Marinate the meat:** Place ⅓ cup marinade into a large ziplock bag, reserving remainder for dressing. Add meat; marinate in the fridge for at least 1 hour, up to overnight.

3. **Prepare pepper mixture:** Heat oil in a large frying pan over medium-high heat. Add onion, garlic, and salt; sauté for 5-8 minutes, until onions have softened and are starting to brown.

4. Turn heat to high; add pepper strips. Cook 3-5 minutes, until peppers are slightly softened but still have some bite. Remove from heat; set aside to cool.

5. **Prepare the meat:** Remove meat from marinade, discarding remaining marinade in bag. Grill or broil meat for 8-10 minutes per side, until it reaches desired level of doneness. For best results, cook until it reaches an internal temperature of about 130°F. Set aside to rest for 10-15 minutes.

6. **Assemble the salad:** Combine lettuce, snow peas, avocado, cooled pepper mixture, and dressing in a large bowl. Top with sliced London broil; toss before serving.

Plan Ahead Dressing can be made a week ahead and stored in the fridge in an airtight container. Steak can be made up to 3 days ahead. For best results, slice fresh before serving. Pepper mixture can also be made up to 3 days ahead and stored in the fridge until ready to serve.

Grilled Chicken and Broccoli Salad

with Roasted Tomato Vinaigrette

Meat | Yield 6-8 servings

This is the kind of salad that's light enough to keep people hungry for the main course, with varied flavors and textures and special enough to impress guests.

2 thinly cut chicken cutlets

DRESSING

1 plum tomato, halved

4 cloves garlic

1 teaspoon + ¼ cup olive oil

1 teaspoon kosher salt, divided

½ teaspoon black pepper, divided

2 Tablespoons balsamic vinegar

3 cubes frozen basil

1 Tablespoon honey

ROASTED BROCCOLI

12 ounces fresh or frozen and defrosted broccoli florets

1 teaspoon kosher salt

¼ teaspoon black pepper

3 Tablespoons olive oil

ASSEMBLY

8 ounces salad greens

1 pint grape or cherry tomatoes, halved

1. **Prepare the dressing:** Preheat oven to 400°F. Place tomato and garlic on a large piece of foil. Drizzle with olive oil; sprinkle with half the salt and pepper. Fold the foil to form a small packet. Place on small baking pan.
2. Bake for 40 minutes. Set aside to cool.
3. Once cooled, carefully open the foil packet; transfer vegetables and juices from inside the foil packet into the jar of a blender. Add remaining oil, salt, pepper, balsamic vinegar, basil, and honey; blend until completely smooth.
4. **Prepare the grilled chicken:** Place chicken cutlets into a bag or bowl; add ¼ cup dressing, reserving the remainder. Place chicken into fridge; marinate for at least 10-20 minutes, preferably a few hours, up to overnight.
5. Preheat grill, grill pan, or broiler. Grill or broil chicken on high for 4-6 minutes per side, or until cooked through. Set aside to cool, then thinly slice or cube.
6. **Prepare the broccoli:** Preheat oven to 400°F. Line a baking sheet with parchment paper.
7. Toss broccoli with salt, pepper, and oil on prepared baking sheet. Bake for 25-30 minutes; set aside to cool.
8. **Assemble the salad:** Add greens to a large salad bowl. Top with grape tomatoes, roasted broccoli, and grilled chicken. Toss with reserved dressing.

Variation This salad is fantastic without the chicken as well, so it can be enjoyed with a pareve meal.

Plan Ahead Dressing can be prepared ahead and stored in the fridge for up to 1 week. Grilled chicken and roasted broccoli can each be prepared a day or two ahead. Store all components separately; assemble salad just before serving.

Crispy Chicken Salad

Meat | Yield 6-8 servings

I was inspired by those popular schnitzel sandwiches that are sold in seemingly every kosher takeout store: crispy breaded chicken, crispy pastrami, topped with lettuce, tomato, and coleslaw. In this recipe, I've made it into a fun salad that's filling and bound to please! It does have a few components to prepare, but it's a perfect special-occasion salad.

CRISPY CHICKEN

1 pound chicken cutlets, cut into bite-size pieces

2 Tablespoons flour

1 egg, lightly beaten

¾ cup cornflake crumbs

CRISPY PASTRAMI

6 ounces sliced pastrami

CREAMY GARLIC DRESSING

½ cup mayonnaise

2 Tablespoons red wine vinegar

6 cloves garlic, minced OR 6 cubes frozen garlic

1 Tablespoon honey

½ teaspoon chili powder

1 teaspoon kosher salt

SALAD

2 cups shredded cabbage

8 ounces romaine lettuce

2 plum tomatoes, diced

1. **Prepare the crispy chicken:** Preheat oven to 400°F. Line 2 baking sheets with parchment paper; coat well with nonstick cooking spray and set aside.
2. Place chicken pieces into a large bowl. Add flour; toss to coat. Add egg; toss until chicken is coated and sticky. Add cornflake crumbs; toss to fully coat all chicken in crumbs.
3. Transfer chicken in a single layer to prepared baking sheets; for maximun crispness, leave some room between pieces. Coat chicken well with nonstick cooking spray.
4. Bake for 10 minutes, until cooked through. Set aside.
5. **Prepare the crispy pastrami:** Line a baking sheet with foil; heat broiler. Place pastrami in a single layer on prepared baking sheet. Broil 2-4 minutes; flip, broil second side 2-4 minutes, until crispy. Set aside to cool, then dice.
6. **Prepare the creamy garlic dressing:** Combine dressing ingredients in a small bowl. Whisk until smooth.
7. **Prepare the cabbage:** Half an hour before serving, toss ¼ cup dressing with cabbage.
8. **Assemble the salad:** Place lettuce, tomatoes, and marinated cabbage into a large bowl. Add crispy chicken and pastrami. Top with remaining dressing; toss to coat.

Note Add your favorite sandwich toppings, such as diced avocado, sliced pickles or fried onions.

Variation Use honey mustard dressing instead of Creamy Garlic Dressing: Combine ½ cup mayo, 2 Tablespoons honey, 2 Tablespoons yellow mustard, and salt and pepper to taste.

Plan Ahead Dressing can be made up to a week ahead. Chicken and pastrami can each be prepared 1-2 days ahead. Assemble just before serving.

Thanksgiving Salad

Meal | Yield 6-8 servings

I was inspired by the flavors and components of a traditional Thanksgiving meal — the butternut squash, the Brussels sprouts, the cranberries, the turkey, and even some croutons to resemble stuffing. The resulting salad is so good, I hope you won't wait for Thanksgiving to make it!

ROASTED VEGETABLES

- 1 (1-pound) bag frozen Brussels sprouts, defrosted
- 1 small butternut squash, diced
- 3 Tablespoons olive oil
- 2 teaspoons kosher salt
- 1 teaspoon chili powder
- ½ teaspoon cinnamon

SALAD

- 12 ounces romaine lettuce
- 6 ounces turkey deli, sliced, diced, or torn
- ½ cup croutons, preferably Caesar-flavored
- ½ cup dried cranberries

DRESSING

- ¼ cup mayonnaise
- 2 Tablespoons olive oil
- 2 Tablespoons apple cider vinegar
- ½ teaspoon kosher salt
- 1 teaspoon garlic powder
- ½ teaspoon dried sage
- ¼ teaspoon black pepper
- 1 Tablespoon pure maple syrup

1. **Prepare the roasted vegetables:** Preheat oven to 425°F. Line 2 baking sheets with parchment paper.
2. Use a paper towel to squeeze as much liquid as possible from defrosted Brussels sprouts. Halve each sprout. Place into a large bowl.
3. Add butternut squash, oil, salt, chili powder, and cinnamon. Toss to coat. Divide between prepared baking sheets.
4. Roast for about 50 minutes, until vegetables are starting to brown. Set aside to cool completely.
5. **Assemble the salad:** Place lettuce, turkey, croutons, cranberries, and roasted vegetables into a large bowl.
6. **Prepare the dressing:** Add all dressing ingredients to a small bowl. Whisk to combine.
7. Pour dressing over salad; toss to combine.

Plan Ahead Roasted vegetables can be prepared up to 2 days ahead of time and stored in the fridge. Dressing can be prepared up to a week ahead of time and refrigerated. Salad should be assembled just before serving.

Mushroom, Tomato, and Quinoa Salad
with Balsamic Shallot Dressing

Pareve | Yield 6 servings

Doesn't it always seem like the best recipes come about by chance? I remember so clearly the first time I made this recipe. I was looking through my fridge for something to eat when I came across some roasted mushrooms and cooked quinoa. A further look yielded some beautiful, colorful heirloom tomatoes. I had a little bit of balsamic dressing left over from a different salad, and I added some shallots to punch up the flavor. And then, as I ate this delicious creation, I remember thinking, This will be an amazing addition one day when I write another cookbook!

MUSHROOMS

24 ounces baby bella mushrooms , sliced

2 Tablespoons olive oil

1½ teaspoons kosher salt

BALSAMIC SHALLOT DRESSING

¼ cup olive oil

3 Tablespoons balsamic vinegar

2 Tablespoons honey

1½ teaspoons kosher salt

3-4 cloves garlic, minced

2 shallots, thinly sliced, raw or caramelized (see Note)

ASSEMBLY

1½ cups raw quinoa, cooked according to package directions

1 pint cherry or grape tomatoes, halved

1. **Prepare the mushrooms:** Preheat oven to 425°F. Line a baking sheet with parchment paper.
2. Place mushrooms, oil, and salt on baking sheet; toss to combine. Roast for about 45 minutes, until browned.
3. **Prepare the balsamic shallot dressing:** Combine all ingredients except shallots in a small bowl. Whisk to combine. Add shallots; marinate for at least 10-15 minutes, up to overnight.
4. **Assemble the salad:** Place quinoa, tomatoes, roasted mushrooms, and dressing into a large bowl. Stir well to combine.

Note Caramelizing the shallots adds an incredible extra layer of flavor, but you can sub in a frozen cube of sautéed onion. To fry shallots, in a frying pan combine 1 Tablespoon oil with 2 large sliced shallots and ½ teaspoon kosher salt. Cook over medium high heat for 8-10 minutes, stirring occasionally, until cooked through and caramelized.

Plan Ahead Salad can be fully prepared up to a day ahead. If making it more in advance, prepare the mushrooms, quinoa, and dressing up to 3 days ahead, store separately in the fridge, and assemble when ready to serve.

Snap Pea, Corn, and Cabbage Salad

Pareve | Yield 6 servings

This easy and healthy salad is reminiscent of light and fresh summer flavors, but it's easy to make year round. Because it's so simple to prepare, it's my go-to recipe for a last-minute salad addition for extra guests!

½ pound sugar snap peas, sliced

kernels from **2** ears of fresh corn

8 ounces red cabbage

8 ounces white cabbage

DRESSING

6 Tablespoons olive oil

zest of **1** lemon

juice of **2** lemons

1½ teaspoons kosher salt

2 cubes frozen basil

1 Tablespoon sugar OR sweetener, optional

1. **Prepare the dressing:** Combine all dressing ingredients in a small bowl. Whisk to combine. Set aside until ready to use.
2. **Prepare the salad:** Place snap peas, corn, red cabbage, and white cabbage into a large bowl. Add desired amount of dressing; toss to combine. Allow to rest for 5-10 minutes for flavors to blend before serving.

Variation To make this recipe year round, use 1 (15.25-ounce) can of corn, drained, in place of the fresh corn.

Plan Ahead Dressing can be prepared up to a week ahead and stored in the fridge until ready to use. Salad should be assembled fresh.

Eggplant and Japanese Yam Salad
with Tahini Dressing

Pareve | Yield 6-8 servings

This salad looks and seems simple, but there's some magic in the combination of flavors and textures that surprises your guests and keeps everyone going back for more!

1 large eggplant, diced

2 teaspoons kosher salt, divided

3 Japanese yams, peeled and diced

¼ cup olive oil

¾ cup fresh parsley, chopped

TAHINI DRESSING

⅓ cup tahini paste

juice of 2 limes

2 Tablespoons olive oil

1 Tablespoon soy sauce

1 teaspoon garlic powder

2 Tablespoons cold water

1. Preheat oven to 425°F. Line 2 baking sheets with parchment paper; set aside.
2. Place eggplant and 1 teaspoon salt into a large bowl. Toss to combine. Let sit for about 10 minutes, then pat dry with paper towels.
3. Add Japanese yams, oil, and remaining teaspoon salt to bowl. Toss to combine. Divide mixture between prepared baking sheets.
4. Bake for 40-50 minutes, stirring halfway through, until vegetables are starting to brown. Set aside to cool completely before assembling.
5. **Meanwhile, prepare tahini dressing:** Combine all dressing ingredients in a small bowl; whisk to combine.
6. Pour dressing over cooled vegetables; add chopped parsley. Toss to combine.

Variation If you can't find Japanese Yams, you can use regular sweet potatoes in their place.

Plan Ahead Vegetables can be roasted and dressing prepared a day or two before serving and assembled fresh. Tahini dressing may thicken in the fridge; add water to reach desired consistency.

Rainbow Salad

Pareve | Yield 6 servings

With almost nothing to prep, I make this recipe when I don't have time, but still want to wow my guests. The combination of sweet and savory flavors, plus all kinds of great crunchy textures, really make this a winner.

MAPLE LIME DRESSING

- ⅓ cup olive oil
- ¼ cup pure maple sy
- 3 Tablespoons lime juice
- 1 clove garlic, minced OR 1 cube frozen garlic
- 1½ teaspoons kosher salt
- pinch cayenne pepper

SALAD

- 8 ounces romaine lettuce
- 4 ounces shredded red cabbage
- 1 mango, diced
- 1 avocado, diced
- ½ cup pomegranate seeds
- 1 cup lightly crushed sweet potato chips
- ¾ cup crispy fried onions (such as French's)

1. **Prepare the dressing:** Whisk together all dressing ingredients in a small bowl until combined. Set aside.
2. Place all salad ingredients in a large bowl. Add dressing just before serving; toss to combine.

Variation When pomegranate seeds are not in season, use dried cranberries or dried cherries instead.

Plan Ahead Dressing can be stored in an airtight container in the fridge for up to 1 week. Salad should be assembled fresh.

Cucumber, Apple, and Radish Salad

Pareve | Yield 6 servings

This started out as a traditional cucumber salad, but then I decided to cut out any sweetener in the dressing and compensate with fresh fruit instead. Then I started adding this and that and before I knew it, I had an instant favorite that got the kind of feedback any cook loves to hear: That burst of sweetness was so unexpected!

4-5 Persian cucumbers, sliced thin

kosher salt

1 large shallot, chopped

1 Granny Smith apple, cut into small thin slices

6 radishes, thinly sliced

½ cup fresh parsley, chopped

½ cup fresh dill, chopped

4 ounces baby arugula

DRESSING

juice of **1** lemon

1 Tablespoon red wine vinegar

2 cloves garlic, minced

1 teaspoon kosher salt

¼ teaspoon black pepper

¼ cup olive oil

1. Place sliced cucumbers into a large salad bowl. Sprinkle with salt, toss, and let sit for 2-3 minutes.
2. Add shallot, apple, radishes, parsley, and dill. Set aside.
3. **Prepare the dressing:** Combine all dressing ingredients in a bowl; whisk to combine.
4. Pour dressing over salad about 10 minutes before serving. Immediately before serving, add arugula; toss to combine.

Plan Ahead Dressing can be prepared up to a week ahead. Salad should be prepared and assembled just before serving.

Sweet and Spicy Citrus Salad

Pareve | Yield 6 Servings

The first time I served this salad, it was gone within minutes. My guests were all in agreement: "You have to put this in the cookbook!" I hesitated. "I don't know," I answered. "It's the kind of salad you have to taste to really appreciate how amazing it is." Everyone thought for a minute and then kinda murmured, "Well, you'll just have to tell them. It's too good to miss." So here it is. Try it, and you'll understand.

DRESSING

1 small carrot, finely minced or ground (see Note)

¼ cup olive oil

1 Tablespoon rice vinegar

2 Tablespoons honey

juice of 1 lemon

½-inch fresh ginger, minced OR 1 cube frozen ginger

3 cloves garlic, minced

1 teaspoon kosher salt

1 teaspoon sriracha

SALAD

4 cups salad greens (I use spring mix)

2 large oranges, peeled and cubed

½ cup dried cranberries

4 scallions, sliced

⅓ cup wasabi peas

1. **Prepare the dressing:** Combine all dressing ingredients in a small bowl. Whisk to combine.
2. **Prepare the salad:** Place all salad ingredients into a large salad bowl. Drizzle with dressing; toss to coat evenly.

Note I prefer a little carrot texture in the dressing, so I grate it on the smallest side of a box grater, but you can use a food processor to process dressing ingredients until smooth.

Plan Ahead Dressing can be prepared up to a week ahead. Salad should be prepared and assembled just before serving.

Asian Broccoli and Quinoa Salad

Pareve | Yield 6-8 Servings

This filling salad recipe is full of color, texture, and flavor. Add some grilled chicken for the ultimate lunch dish, or prepare it for a summer shalosh seudos meal that your family and friends will love.

1¼ cups raw quinoa

1 pound fresh or frozen broccoli florets, cut into bite-size pieces

1 red bell pepper, diced

¼-½ pound snow peas, ends trimmed, halved

2 scallions, thinly sliced

DRESSING

¼ cup toasted sesame oil

2½ Tablespoons rice vinegar

4 teaspoons soy sauce

4 teaspoons honey

1 teaspoon kosher salt

1 teaspoon garlic powder

½ teaspoon ground ginger

1. Cook quinoa according to package directions; set aside to cool.
2. Cook broccoli in salted, boiling water for 2-3 minutes, until slightly tender. Drain; shock in ice water to stop the cooking. Remove from ice water after 2 minutes; set aside.
3. In a large bowl, toss together pepper, snow peas, scallions, and broccoli. Add the cooked quinoa.
4. **Prepare the dressing:** Whisk together all dressing ingredients in a small bowl.
5. Add dressing to veggie and quinoa mixture; toss to combine and evenly distribute all ingredients.

Plan Ahead Dressing can be prepared up to a week ahead and stored in the fridge. Quinoa and broccoli can be prepared 2-3 days ahead. For best results, salad should be assembled within an hour or two of serving.

Slow-Roasted Jalapeño and Garlic Dip

Pareve | Yield 1½-2 cups

This recipe comes from my brother Mordy, who is known in my family for amazing dips (and the world's best sautéed liver!). Cooking the garlic and jalapeño slowly like this makes it incredibly flavorful — and make sure to savor that delicious oil, too!

- **¾ cup** olive oil, divided
- **1 cup** garlic cloves, sliced
- **5** jalapeño peppers, cut into thin half-rings (see Note)
- **1½ teaspoons** kosher salt

1. Heat about 1 tablespoon oil in a small pot over high heat.
2. Add garlic, jalapeños, and salt; stir to combine. Cook, stirring almost constantly, for about 2 minutes, until mixture is starting to brown.
3. Turn the heat to low. Add remaining oil. Cook for about 45 minutes, stirring every 15 minutes, until the garlic is golden and the jalapeños have browned. Watch toward the end to ensure it doesn't burn.

Note Depending on how hot you like your food, you can remove some or all of the membrane and seeds from the jalapeño. Remember that the more you leave in, the hotter it'll be.

Plan Ahead This dip will keep in an airtight container in the fridge for about 1 week.

Sweet Onion and Mushroom Dip

Pareve | Yield about 4 cups

The sweetness of the onions pairs so well with the savory mushrooms, resulting in a dip that's bound to become a family favorite.

3 Tablespoons olive oil

2 large Spanish onions, finely diced

1 teaspoon kosher salt

20-24 ounces baby bella mushrooms, finely diced

2 cloves garlic, minced

2 teaspoons red wine vinegar

1 teaspoon soy sauce

2 Tablespoons brown sugar

1 cup mayonnaise

1. Heat oil in a large, deep frying pan over low heat. Add onions and salt. Cook, stirring occasionally, for 15-20 minutes, until onions start to get some color.

2. Add mushrooms, garlic, vinegar, soy sauce, and brown sugar; stir to combine. Raise heat to medium-low; cook for 30-40 minutes, stirring occasionally, until the color has deepened. Set aside to cool completely before continuing.

3. Mix cooled onion and mushroom mixture with mayonnaise. Store in fridge until ready to serve.

Variation For a sweet onion dip, omit the mushrooms and double the onions instead.

Plan Ahead The finished dip can't be frozen, but you can freeze the onion and mushroom mixture, then defrost and mix with mayonnaise before serving.

PORTOBELLO LENTIL SOUP, PAGE 100

ROASTED VEGETABLE SOUP, PAGE 94

ZUCCHINI BEEF AND BARLEY STEW, PAGE 108

SPICY CARROT ASPARAGUS SOUP, PAGE 102

RICH AND CREAMY PEA SOUP, PAGE 90

HEARTY AUTUMN VEGETABLE SOUP, PAGE 92

Soups *and* Stews

Rich and Creamy Pea Soup

Meat or Pareve | Yield 8-10 servings

One of my favorite quick comfort food hacks is to add fresh or frozen vegetables to a package of split pea soup mix. On one chilly day, in the mood for soup, I found some frozen peas in my freezer, and some split pea soup mix in the pantry. I thought ... why not put those together? The resulting soup was so creamy and delicious that I played around with the recipe, made it even better, and knew I had a cookbook-worthy dish! Using a marrow bone adds incredible richness to make this soup that much more enjoyable.

¼ cup oil

1 large onion, diced

2 teaspoons kosher salt, divided

2 (1-pound) bags frozen green (sweet) peas

3 cloves garlic, minced

1 marrow bone (optional)

2 (6-ounce) packages split pea soup mix, flavor packets discarded

4 cups vegetable, chicken, OR beef broth

4 cups water

1. Heat oil in a large soup pot over medium heat. Add onion and 1 teaspoon salt. Cook, stirring occasionally, for about 5 minutes, until onions are translucent.
2. Add frozen peas, garlic, and marrow bone (if using). Cook, stirring occasionally, for about 10 minutes, until softened.
3. Add split peas, broth, water, and remaining teaspoon salt.
4. Cover; bring to a boil. Reduce heat and simmer for at least 1 hour, preferably 2 hours (to increase flavor). If using marrow bone, remove from soup, add marrow back into soup, and discard bone.
5. Using an immersion blender, blend for 2-3 minutes, until smooth and very creamy.

Plan Ahead This soup freezes well in an airtight container.

Note You can omit the marrow bone and use vegetable broth for a pareve soup option.

Hearty Autumn Vegetable Soup

Pareve | Yield 6-8 servings

This soup is a true hearty comfort food; ever since it first appeared on my blog it's been immensely popular with readers all over the world.

- **3 Tablespoons** olive oil
- **2** Spanish onions
- **2 large** carrots
- **6-8 stalks** celery
- **1** parsnip
- **1** sweet potato
- **2-3 cloves** garlic, finely minced
- **1 (28-ounce) can** crushed tomatoes
- **1 (15-ounce) can** chickpeas, drained and rinsed
- **¼ cup** fresh parsley, chopped
- **4 cups** vegetable broth
- **6 cups** water
- **4 teaspoons** kosher salt
- **¼ teaspoon** black pepper

1. Peel and dice all vegetables.
2. Heat oil in a large soup pot over medium-low heat.
3. Add onions, carrots, and celery. Stir; cook over medium-low heat for about 10 minutes, stirring occasionally, until vegetables are slightly softened and aromatic.
4. Add remaining ingredients; bring to a boil.
5. Reduce heat to low; simmer, uncovered, for about 2 hours, until vegetables are tender and liquid has thickened. Watch to ensure that too much liquid doesn't boil away. If needed, add additional water to bring soup to desired consistency.

Plan Ahead This soup can be prepared ahead and frozen in an airtight container.

Roasted Vegetable Soup

Pareve | Yield 6-8 servings

What started out as a fridge full of produce that had to be used up has morphed into one of my all-time favorite soups. Roasting the vegetables brings out their flavors, resulting in a healthy soup that's packed with flavor and so filling! Feel free to customize your soup based on whichever veggies you happen to have on hand.

ROASTED VEGETABLES

2 large zucchini, diced

3 medium yellow squash, diced

2 red bell peppers, diced

2 onions, diced

1 pound frozen cauliflower florets, defrosted

¼ cup oil

1 Tablespoon kosher salt

½ teaspoon black pepper

SOUP

4 cups vegetable broth

about **6 cups** water

2 bay leaves

1 Tablespoon kosher salt

1. **Prepare the roasted vegetables:** Preheat oven to 400°F. Line 2 baking sheets with parchment paper.
2. Place vegetables, oil, salt, and pepper into a bowl. Toss to combine. Divide between prepared baking sheets. Roast for 50-60 minutes, until vegetables are starting to brown.
3. **Prepare the soup:** Place roasted vegetables, along with any juices, into a large soup pot. Add soup ingredients; bring to a boil.
4. Simmer for about 1 hour. Discard bay leaves. Using an immersion blender, blend soup well, for about 3 minutes, until fully smooth. Adjust salt and pepper to taste.

Plan Ahead This soup can be prepared ahead and frozen in an airtight container.

Moroccan Cauliflower Soup

Pareve | Yield 8 servings

I was once eating out with my sisters, and we all ordered soup that was new to us. After just a quick taste, we kind of looked at each other and knew that I'd be recreating it at home. The resulting soup was so hearty, so flavorful, and so satisfying, it was a no-brainer to include it here!

2 Tablespoons oil

2 Spanish onions, diced

1 Tablespoon kosher salt, divided

1 red bell pepper, diced

3 cloves garlic, minced

1 (14.5-ounce) can diced tomatoes, preferably fire roasted

2 (12-ounce) bags riced cauliflower

1½ teaspoons cumin

1 teaspoon chili powder

1 teaspoon smoked paprika

1 (6-ounce) can tomato paste

2 teaspoons dried parsley

1. Heat oil in a large pot over medium heat. Add onions, 1 teaspoon salt, pepper, and garlic. Sauté, stirring occasionally, for about 10 minutes, until softened and fragrant.
2. Add diced tomatoes with their liquid, cauliflower, cumin, chili powder, paprika, and remaining 2 teaspoons salt. Cook for an additional 10 minutes.
3. Add tomato paste, dried parsley, and enough water to cover all the vegetables. Cover; bring to a boil; reduce heat to low and simmer for 1-2 hours, until thickened.

Plan Ahead This soup freezes well in an airtight container.

Creamy Broccoli Leek Soup

Pareve | Yield 8-10 servings

Inspired by the perennially popular potato leek soup, I set out to make a healthy, vegetable-packed version of that soup for a treat that's as healthy as it is tasty. This satisfying soup totally fits the bill!

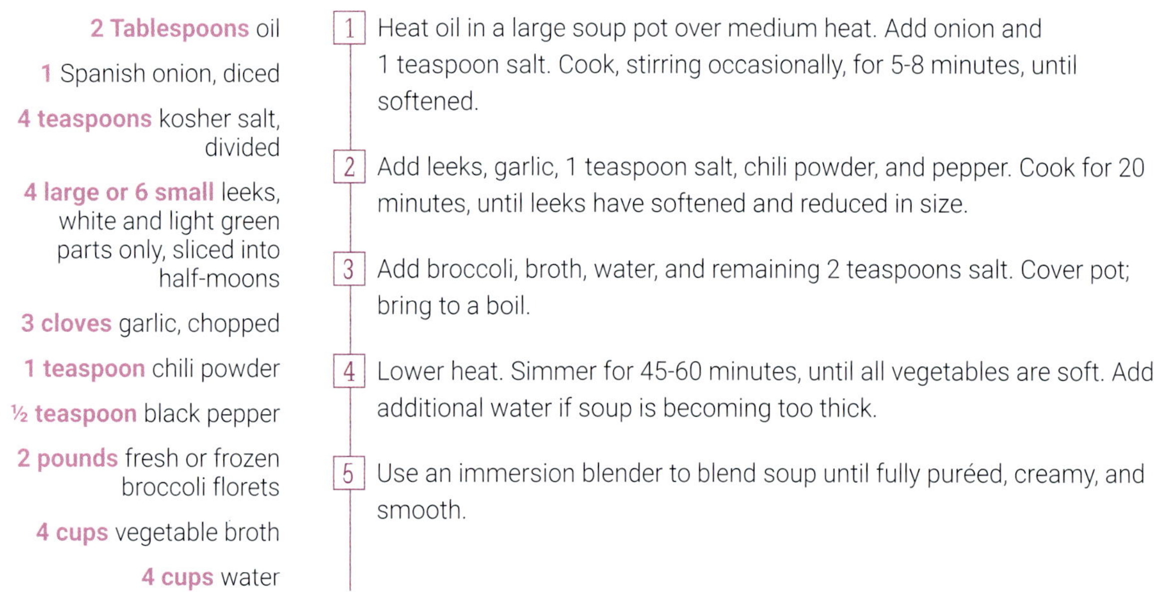

2 Tablespoons oil

1 Spanish onion, diced

4 teaspoons kosher salt, divided

4 large or 6 small leeks, white and light green parts only, sliced into half-moons

3 cloves garlic, chopped

1 teaspoon chili powder

½ teaspoon black pepper

2 pounds fresh or frozen broccoli florets

4 cups vegetable broth

4 cups water

1. Heat oil in a large soup pot over medium heat. Add onion and 1 teaspoon salt. Cook, stirring occasionally, for 5-8 minutes, until softened.
2. Add leeks, garlic, 1 teaspoon salt, chili powder, and pepper. Cook for 20 minutes, until leeks have softened and reduced in size.
3. Add broccoli, broth, water, and remaining 2 teaspoons salt. Cover pot; bring to a boil.
4. Lower heat. Simmer for 45-60 minutes, until all vegetables are soft. Add additional water if soup is becoming too thick.
5. Use an immersion blender to blend soup until fully puréed, creamy, and smooth.

Plan Ahead Soup can be prepared and frozen in an airtight container until ready to use.

Portobello Lentil Soup

Pareve | Yield 8 servings

In the world of plant-based food, both mushrooms and lentils are often used as a stand-in for meat and traditional proteins. It's no wonder, then, that this soup, filled with both of these ingredients, is one of the most filling soups I've ever made, despite being pareve and even vegan.

3 Tablespoons oil

2 onions, diced

4 teaspoons kosher salt, divided

6 portobello mushrooms, diced

1 (8-12-ounce) package baby bella mushrooms, diced

1 teaspoon dried parsley

1 teaspoon dried thyme

4 cloves garlic, minced

1 pound dried lentils

4 cups vegetable broth

4 cups water

1 Tablespoon red wine vinegar

1. Soak lentils overnight. Drain.

2. In a large soup pot, heat oil over medium heat. Add onions and 1 teaspoon salt. Sauté for about 10 minutes, until softened.

2. Add both types of mushrooms, 1 teaspoon salt, parsley, thyme, and garlic. Cook for 10 minutes, until mushrooms have reduced in size.

3. Add lentils, broth, water, and remaining 2 teaspoons salt. Cover pot; bring mixture to a boil. Reduce heat; simmer for 2 hours, until the lentils are soft. Remove from heat; stir in vinegar just before serving.

Plan Ahead This soup freezes well in an airtight container.

Spicy Carrot Asparagus Soup

Pareve | Yield 6-8 servings

I've been making this wonderful soup for a couple of years now, and always enjoyed the combination of sweet carrots and savory asparagus. One day, on a whim, I added a pinch of cayenne pepper and discovered how much that addition takes the flavor to another level. If you don't like things spicy, simply omit the cayenne pepper.

2 Tablespoons oil
2 onions, diced
4 cloves garlic, minced
2 teaspoons kosher salt, divided
5 carrots, peeled and sliced
1 pound asparagus, fresh or frozen, chopped
¼ teaspoon cayenne pepper
¼ teaspoon ground ginger
4 cups vegetable broth
4 cups water

1. Heat oil in a large pot over medium heat. Add onions, garlic, and 1 teaspoon salt. Cook, stirring occasionally, for 8-10 minutes, until vegetables have softened.
2. Add carrots, asparagus, cayenne pepper, ginger, and remaining teaspoon salt. Cook for 10 minutes, until softened.
3. Add broth and water to cover (about 4 cups). Cover pot; bring to a boil. Reduce heat; simmer for about 1 hour.
4. Use an immersion blender to blend soup well, until very creamy. Be aware that because of the stringy texture of the asparagus, this soup needs extra blending time in order to eliminate any stringiness.

Plan Ahead This soup freezes well in an airtight container.

Crockpot Minestrone Chicken Soup

Meat | Yield 6-8 servings

You know what's better than a soup that's a full meal in a bowl? A hearty and delicious soup that's not only a meal in a bowl, but also cooks in a crockpot all day so you don't even need to think about dinner!

3 Tablespoons oil

1 onion, diced

4 teaspoons kosher salt, divided

3 large carrots, diced

1 head celery, diced

3 cloves garlic, minced

4 dark chicken cutlets (about 1½ pounds)

2 (15-ounce) cans kidney beans, drained and rinsed

1 (28-ounce) can diced tomatoes

1 (6-ounce) can tomato paste

1 Tablespoon dried parsley

1 teaspoon dried oregano

½ teaspoon dried thyme

½ cup small pasta, such as elbows, optional

1. Heat oil in a large, deep frying pan over medium heat. Add onion and 1 teaspoon salt. Cook, stirring occasionally, for about 5 minutes, until softened.
2. Add carrots, celery, garlic, and 1 teaspoon salt. Cook, stirring occasionally, for 8-10 minutes, until softened.
3. Place sautéed vegetables into crockpot. Add chicken, beans, diced tomatoes with their liquid, tomato paste, remaining 2 teaspoons salt, parsley, oregano, and thyme. Add water to cover.
4. Cook on low for 6-8 hours or on high for 4-6 hours. If desired, add pasta during the last 20 minutes of cooking.
5. Before serving, remove chicken from soup and cut or shred into bite-size pieces. Return chicken to soup; stir to distribute.

Variation Instead of using a crockpot, sauté the vegetables in a large pot, then add remaining ingredients. Bring to a boil over high heat; reduce heat and simmer on low for about 2 hours, until vegetables have softened and chicken is cooked through.

Plan Ahead This soup freezes well in an airtight container. For best results, follow stovetop variation if you're planning to freeze the soup. Cook without pasta; add cooked pasta when reheating.

Meaty Root Vegetable Soup

Meat | Yield 6 servings

This soup is rich, creamy, and the ultimate comfort food. You may want to serve some crusty bread with it. You're going to find your family begging for this soup again and again.

- **2 Tablespoons** oil
- **2** Spanish onions, diced
- **2 teaspoons** kosher salt, divided
- **3** parsnips, peeled and cut into chunks
- **1 large** carrot, peeled and cut into chunks
- **1** sweet potato, peeled and cut into chunks
- **1** Fuji apple, peeled and cut into chunks
- **1 clove** garlic, minced
- **1 cube** frozen ginger
- **2 cubes** frozen dill
- **1-2 pounds** kolichel
- **2-3** marrow bones
- **8 cups** water
- root vegetable chips (such as Terra Chips), crushed, for garnish (optional)

1. In a large soup pot, heat oil over medium heat. Add onions and 1 teaspoon salt; cook for 5-8 minutes, until translucent.
2. Add parsnips, carrot, sweet potato, apple, remaining teaspoon salt, garlic, ginger, and dill; cook for 5-10 minutes, until fragrant.
3. Add meat, marrow bones, and water. Cover; bring to a boil, then reduce heat and simmer, loosely covered, for 2-3 hours. Remove meat and marrow bones (I cook them in a net bag to make them easier to remove). Scoop marrow from the bones; add marrow into the soup. Use an immersion blender to blend soup for about 3 minutes, until completely creamy. Shred meat; add to soup.
4. Garnish with crushed chips just before serving.

Variation Instead of kolichel, use bone-in flanken.

Plan Ahead This soup freezes well in an airtight container.

Zucchini Beef and Barley Stew

Meat | Yield 10-12 servings

I originally made this soup for my father's birthday party. I love it when I can make one dish that everyone — from my father right on down to my infant nephew — will enjoy, no matter their diet or personal preference. This thick and hearty soup is a meal-in-a-bowl that epitomizes homemade comfort food.

MEAT

oil, for searing

1½ pounds beef stew meat, cut into bite-size chunks

1 teaspoon kosher salt

½ teaspoon black pepper

SOUP

1 Tablespoon oil

1 Spanish onion, diced

2 Tablespoons kosher salt, divided

4 cloves garlic, minced

6 stalks celery, diced

5 large zucchini, quartered and cut into chunks

3 Tablespoons tomato paste

2 cubes frozen basil

1 Tablespoon dried parsley

½ teaspoon black pepper

¾ cup barley, rinsed

10 cups water

1. **Prepare the meat:** Heat oil over high heat in a large soup pot. Sprinkle salt and pepper over meat; sear for about 1 minute per side, until browned. Work in batches to avoid overcrowding. Set meat aside.
2. **Prepare the soup:** In the same pot, heat oil over medium heat. Add onion and 1 teaspoon salt. Sauté for 5-8 minutes, until softened.
3. Add garlic, celery, and 1 teaspoon salt. Cook for 5 minutes.
4. Add zucchini and 1 teaspoon salt. Cook for about 10 minutes, until zucchini has softened.
5. Add reserved meat, tomato paste, basil, parsley, pepper, remaining 1 tablespoon salt, and water.
6. Raise heat to high; cover soup; bring to a boil. Reduce heat to a simmer, then simmer for 1½ hours.
7. Add barley and more water, if needed. Simmer for 1½ hours, until meat and barley are both tender. Taste; adjust salt and pepper, as needed.

Plan Ahead This soup freezes well in an airtight container.

SWEET AND TANGY LEMON POPPERS, PAGE 136

ORANGE SESAME KEBABS, PAGE 142

ROASTED GARLIC STRIP STEAK, PAGE 162

SWEET AND SOUR CABBAGE BRAISED FLANKEN, PAGE 152

SPICE-RUBBED CHICKEN THIGHS, PAGE 118

CROCKPOT PINEAPPLE PEPPER STEAK, PAGE 148

Meat *and* Poultry

Braised Onion Chicken

Meat | Yield 4-6 servings

I've always enjoyed a good one-pot, stovetop chicken recipe — perfect for those times when the oven is otherwise occupied or it's too hot in the kitchen to turn on the oven. For its deceptively complex flavors, this dish relies on the simple — yet incredible and varied — flavors of onions in their many forms.

CHICKEN

- 6-8 pieces chicken, bone-in, skin-on
- oil
- kosher salt, for sprinkling
- black pepper, for sprinkling

SAUCE

- 2 Tablespoons oil
- 1 Spanish onion, sliced
- 1 white onion, sliced
- 1 red onion, sliced
- 1 teaspoon kosher salt
- 2 large shallots, sliced
- 4 cloves garlic, sliced
- 1 teaspoon dried oregano
- ½ teaspoon sage
- about 24 pearl onions, blanched and peeled, optional but recommended (see Note)
- 1 cup white wine OR broth

1. Heat oil in a large pot or Dutch oven over high heat. Sprinkle salt and pepper over both sides of the chicken, then sear for 1-2 minutes per side, until browned. Set aside.
2. **Prepare the sauce:** Reduce heat to medium-low. To the same pot, add oil, Spanish onions, white onion, red onion, and salt. Cook, stirring occasionally, for about 5 minutes, until softened.
3. Add shallots, garlic, oregano, and sage. Continue to cook for 5-8 minutes, until fragrant.
4. Add chicken to the pot, covering it with the onion mixture. Add pearl onions; add wine.
5. Cover pot; bring mixture to a boil. Reduce heat; simmer for 75-90 minutes, until chicken is tender and cooked through.

Plan Ahead Chicken can be cooked a day or two ahead and rewarmed in the sauce, covered, until heated through.

Note Pearl onions add a phenomenal burst of flavor and texture, and they are really easy to prepare. Cut off and discard the root ends, then cook in boiling water for 1 minute. Drain; pour ice water into pot to shock them and stop cooking. Remove onions from the water, and squeeze by the top (opposite the root). The peel will remain in your hands and the center should pop right out.

Middle Eastern Sheet Pan Chicken Dinner

Meat | Yield 4-6 servings

Who doesn't love a good sheet pan dinner? Stick everything on a pan, bake it, and a full dinner – protein, starch and vegetable – is done! This version is packed with flavor thanks to the Middle Eastern spices, and comes together in just minutes. A true go-to dinner.

- **1 Tablespoon** zaatar
- **1 teaspoon** cumin
- **1 teaspoon** kosher salt
- **1 teaspoon** chili powder
- **1 teaspoon** garlic powder
- **½ teaspoon** coriander
- **2 Tablespoons** red wine vinegar
- **6 Tablespoons** olive oil
- **4** Idaho potatoes, peeled and cubed
- **16-20 ounces** cauliflower florets, fresh or frozen, cut into bite-size pieces
- **4-6** chicken bottoms

1. Preheat oven to 425°F. Line a baking sheet with parchment paper; set aside.
2. Combine all spices with vinegar and oil in a large bowl.
3. Place potatoes and cauliflower on baking sheet; add about one-third of the spice and oil mixture. Toss until vegetables are fully coated, then spread in a single layer.
4. Add chicken to bowl with remaining spice and oil mixture. Turn chicken to fully coat on all sides. Arrange chicken over vegetables on baking sheet, leaving space between pieces for even cooking.
5. Bake for about 55 minutes, until chicken is cooked through and vegetables are crispy.

Note Instead of chicken bottoms, you can use your favorite cut of bone-in, skin-on chicken. Adjust baking time as needed for larger or smaller pieces.

Plan Ahead This dish is best enjoyed fresh. You can prepare it the night before and refrigerate, raw. Bake just before serving.

Sticky Blueberry Chicken

Meat | Yield 6-8 servings

I don't often make sticky, sweet chicken recipes, but when I do, they've got to be finger-lickin' good, super-fast to make, and a hit with the whole family. The unique flavors of this recipe certainly fit that bill!

6-8 chicken bottoms

SAUCE

- **¾ cup** blueberry jam
- **½ cup** ketchup
- **2 Tablespoons** Dijon mustard
- **2 Tablespoons** apple cider vinegar
- **2 cloves** garlic, minced
- **2 cubes** frozen basil
- **2 Tablespoons** honey
- **1 Tablespoon** soy sauce
- **1 teaspoon** kosher salt

1. Preheat oven to 425°F. Line a baking sheet with parchment paper; set aside.
2. In a large bowl, whisk together all sauce ingredients until smooth. Add chicken; toss until all pieces are fully coated. For best results, if time allows, set aside to marinate in the fridge for 1-2 hours, up to overnight.
3. Place chicken pieces, skin-side down, on prepared baking sheet, leaving space between them. Do not overlap. Reserve remaining sauce.
4. Bake for 30 minutes; flip each piece over. Brush each chicken bottom generously with reserved sauce. Return to oven; bake for 35-40 minutes, until chicken is cooked through.

Plan Ahead This chicken is best enjoyed fresh, but if necessary, it can be made a day or two ahead and reheated, loosely covered, until warmed through.

Spice-Rubbed Chicken Thighs

Meat | Yield 4-6 servings

This is my ultimate go-to, no-time-to-cook-dinner meal. It's so simple, yet there's perfection in simplicity that makes this chicken just so irresistible. Make double or triple the spice mix so you'll have it ready for next time.

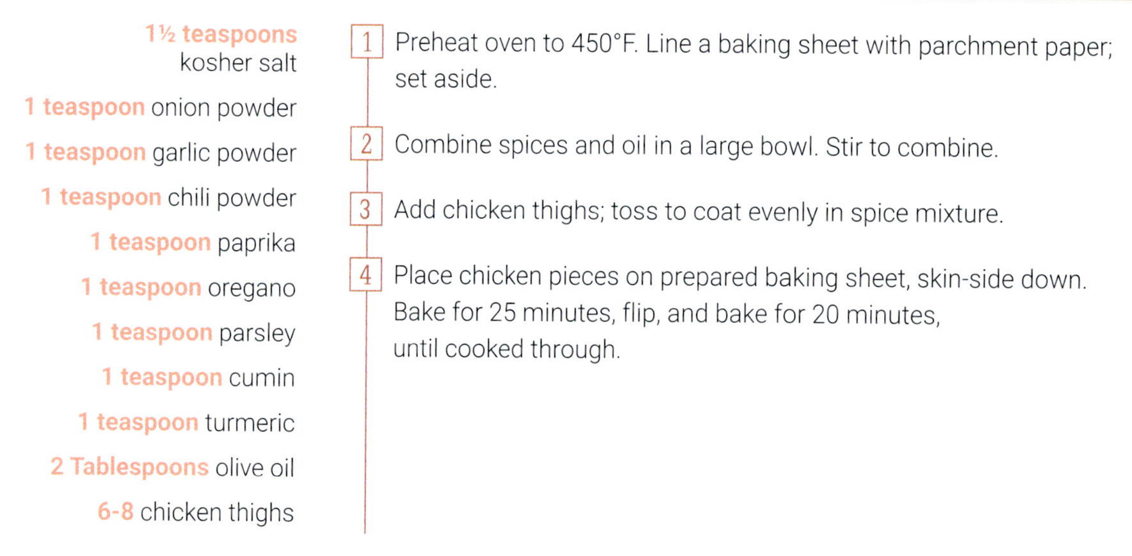

- **1½ teaspoons** kosher salt
- **1 teaspoon** onion powder
- **1 teaspoon** garlic powder
- **1 teaspoon** chili powder
- **1 teaspoon** paprika
- **1 teaspoon** oregano
- **1 teaspoon** parsley
- **1 teaspoon** cumin
- **1 teaspoon** turmeric
- **2 Tablespoons** olive oil
- **6-8** chicken thighs

1. Preheat oven to 450°F. Line a baking sheet with parchment paper; set aside.
2. Combine spices and oil in a large bowl. Stir to combine.
3. Add chicken thighs; toss to coat evenly in spice mixture.
4. Place chicken pieces on prepared baking sheet, skin-side down. Bake for 25 minutes, flip, and bake for 20 minutes, until cooked through.

Plan Ahead This chicken is best enjoyed fresh. If necessary, it can be baked a day or two ahead of time and rewarmed, uncovered, until heated through.

Smoky Maple Drumsticks

Meat | Yield 6 servings

This unexpected gem stole the show at a family BBQ, so I instantly knew that I would save the recipe for my cookbook. I adapted this to an oven-friendly version so I could keep making it all year long, but try it this summer on the grill too! (See Variation.)

- **¾ cup** tomato purée
- **2 Tablespoons** pure maple syrup
- **2 Tablespoons** apple cider vinegar
- **1 teaspoon** kosher salt
- **2 teaspoons** hot sauce
- **1 teaspoon** dried oregano
- **1 teaspoon** smoked paprika
- **12-15** drumsticks

1. Preheat oven to 400°F. Line a baking sheet with foil, coat well with nonstick cooking spray. Set aside.
2. In a large bowl, whisk together all ingredients except chicken until combined. Add chicken; toss until all pieces are fully coated. If time allows, set aside to marinate in the fridge for 1-2 hours, up to overnight.
3. Place drumsticks on prepared baking sheet. Bake for 40 minutes, then turn oven to broil. Broil the drumsticks for about 2 minutes per side, until browned.

Variation Instead of baking these drumsticks in the oven, they can be grilled for a fabulous smoky flavor! Grill on medium heat for 30-35 minutes per side, until cooked through.

Plan Ahead This chicken is best enjoyed fresh, but you can prepare the sauce and chicken and freeze before baking. Defrost; bake fresh.

Apple and Honey Stuffed Chicken

Meat | Yield 6 servings

Friday-night dinner in my parents' home always involved a whole roasted chicken, which is why I now associate it with Shabbos dinner. This beautiful and savory version is inspired by the flavors of fall and Rosh Hashanah, but don't let that stop you from enjoying it every week of the year, starting your own Friday-night tradition.

- 1 Spanish onion, sliced
- 1 (2-4-pound) chicken
- kosher salt, to taste
- black pepper, to taste

GLAZE

- 2 Tablespoons olive oil
- 2 Tablespoons honey
- 1 clove garlic, minced
- 1 teaspoon kosher salt
- ½ teaspoon dried sage
- ½ teaspoon dried thyme
- juice of ½ lemon

FILLING

- 1 Granny Smith apple, peel on, sliced
- 2 shallots, sliced
- 4 cloves garlic, chopped
- ½ lemon, cut into small chunks

1. Preheat oven to 400°F.
2. **Prepare the glaze:** In a small bowl, whisk together all glaze ingredients. Set aside.
3. **Prepare the chicken:** Place sliced onions into a roasting pan.
4. Sprinkle salt and pepper into chicken cavity; place chicken into roasting pan over onions.
5. **Prepare the filling:** Combine apple, shallots, garlic, and lemon in a bowl. Add 2 tablespoons prepared glaze; toss to combine. Fill chicken cavity with this mixture, placing any excess in pan around the chicken.
6. Rub remaining glaze all over chicken. For best results, spoon some under the skin so the flavors are absorbed.
7. Cover; bake for 45 minutes. Uncover; bake for about 45 minutes, until cooked through.

Plan Ahead This chicken is best enjoyed fresh, but it can be baked a day or two ahead of time and reheated, loosely covered, until warmed through.

Garlic Dijon Spatchcock Chicken

with Crispy Potatoes

Meat | Yield 4-6 servings

The garlic Dijon sauce here is DYNAMITE! It's so packed with flavor, and works on almost anything. You can use this sauce however you like; it's great on various cuts of chicken, over salmon, as a marinade for grilled chicken cutlets or steak, and it's the perfect flavoring for roasted vegetables!

GARLIC DIJON SAUCE

- ⅓ cup olive oil
- ¼ cup Dijon mustard
- 15 cloves garlic
- 2 Tablespoons red wine vinegar
- 1 Tablespoon pure maple syrup
- 1 teaspoon kosher salt
- ½ teaspoon black pepper
- 1 teaspoon dried parsley

CHICKEN AND POTATOES

- 1 whole (4-5-pound) chicken, spatchcocked (see Note)
- 6 Yukon Gold potatoes, peeled and cubed
- 2 Tablespoons oil
- 1 teaspoon kosher salt

1. Preheat oven to 400°F. Line 2 baking sheets with parchment paper; set aside.
2. **Prepare the garlic Dijon sauce:** Combine all sauce ingredients in a large container. Use an immersion blender to blend mixture until fully smooth. This can also be done with a food processor or traditional blender.
3. **Prepare the chicken and potatoes:** Reserve about one-quarter of the garlic Dijon sauce. Rub the remainder all over the chicken. For best results, rub some sauce under the skin of the chicken as well.
4. Place chicken on 1 prepared baking sheet. Set aside.
5. Place cubed potatoes on second prepared baking sheet. Toss with oil, salt, and reserved garlic Dijon sauce to coat all potatoes evenly.
6. Bake chicken for about 60 minutes, until cooked through. Bake potatoes for 30-40 minutes. If desired, add to pan with chicken for the last few minutes of baking to absorb chicken flavor.

Note Many butchers will spatchcock a chicken for you, but it's easy to prepare. Use kitchen shears to slice along and remove the backbone, then flatten chicken and place cut-side down on baking sheet.

Variation Use chicken quarters instead of a spatchcocked chicken. The garlic Dijon sauce is also great on roasted vegetables, instead of, or in addition to, the potatoes.

Plan Ahead Garlic Dijon sauce can be prepared up to a week ahead. Chicken and potatoes are best fresh, but they can be baked a day ahead if need be.

Honey Balsamic Baby Chicken Roll-Ups

Meat | Yield 6-8 servings

This recipe was originally created when my sister had a baby early one Friday morning, and I found myself rushing to put Shabbos together for my parents, her family, and other family members at the last minute, with an hour trip in each direction to visit the new mama. Naturally, everything I cooked had to be really easy, but still nice enough for a Shabbos meal. This chicken stole the show – all of it was polished off before we rushed to eat and get ready for a Shalom Zachor!

SAUCE

- ⅓ cup balsamic vinegar
- ⅓ cup honey
- 3 Tablespoons olive oil
- 1 teaspoon kosher salt
- 1 teaspoon garlic powder
- 1 teaspoon dried basil

CHICKEN

- 12 pieces baby chicken (dark chicken cutlets)
- 2 Tablespoons oil
- 1 large Spanish onion, sliced
- 1 teaspoon kosher salt
- ¾ cup cornflake crumbs

1. **Prepare the sauce:** Whisk together all sauce ingredients in a large bowl. Reserve ⅓ cup sauce, then add chicken to the remainder. Place in fridge to marinate for at least 1 hour, up to overnight.
2. Heat oil over medium heat in a large frying pan. Add onion and salt; sauté, stirring occasionally, until onions have softened and are starting to brown, about 10 minutes. Set aside until cool enough to handle before continuing.
3. **Assemble the roll-ups:** Preheat oven to 350°F. Prepare a 9x13-inch roasting pan.
4. Remove one piece of chicken from the marinade. Place a spoonful of onions in the center; roll chicken around the onions and place into prepared pan. Repeat with remaining chicken and onions. Pour any remaining marinade over the chicken.
5. Cover pan tightly; bake for 45 minutes.
6. Meanwhile, combine reserved sauce with crumbs; stir until the it forms a damp mixture similar in texture to wet sand.
7. After 45 minutes, raise oven temperature to 400°F. Uncover chicken; top each piece with some of the crumbs. Return to oven and bake for 30 minutes, until crumbs are crispy.

Note I originally made this recipe without the sautéed onions. They definitely add great flavor to the chicken, but if you're pressed for time, you can skip that step for an even easier dish.

Plan Ahead This can be prepared a day or two ahead and reheated. The roll-ups can also be frozen but the crumbs will not be crispy when reheated. Reheat loosely covered.

Grilled Chicken 2 Ways

Meat | Yield 6-8 servings

Here are two of my easy, go-to ways to marinate chicken for grilling. Go for Basil Lime when you're in a sweet and savory mood, and opt for Herb Mayo when you're in the mood for something light, herbaceous, and extra juicy!

1. Combine all ingredients for desired marinade in a large bowl. Stir to combine.
2. Add chicken; marinate in fridge for at least 1 hour, up to overnight.
3. Remove chicken from marinade; discard any remaining marinade. Using a grill pan, over high heat, broil or grill chicken for about 6 minutes per side, until cooked through.

BASIL LIME MARINADE:

juice of **2** limes

2 Tablespoons olive oil

1 Tablespoon honey

3 cubes frozen basil

5 cloves garlic, minced

1 teaspoon kosher salt

1 teaspoon hot sauce

2-3 pounds dark or white chicken cutlets, cut or pounded thin

HERB MAYO MARINADE

⅔ cup mayonnaise
juice of **1** lemon
1 teaspoon kosher salt
1 teaspoon garlic powder
1 teaspoon onion powder
1 teaspoon dried basil
1 teaspoon dried oregano
1 teaspoon dried thyme
1 teaspoon dried sage
1 teaspoon dried parsley
2-3 pounds dark or white chicken cutlets, cut or pounded thin

Note Prepare extra herb mayo when using that marinade. Store separately and serve alongside the chicken as a dipping sauce.

Plan Ahead Chicken can be prepared ahead and frozen in the marinade. Defrost and grill just before serving.

Zucchini-Wrapped Chicken Strips

Meat | Yield 4-6 servings

These fun-to-eat chicken strips are not just a yummy way to add veggies to your meal — the zucchini actually keeps the chicken soft and juicy!

1½ pounds chicken cutlets, cut into strips

2 large zucchini, cut into long, thin strips

MARINADE

¼ cup honey

⅓ cup mustard

2 Tablespoons oil

2 teaspoons soy sauce

1 teaspoon hot sauce

1 teaspoon garlic powder

1 teaspoon dried parsley

1. In a large bowl, whisk together all marinade ingredients until smooth. Add chicken and zucchini strips; stir to cover all sides.
2. Marinate mixture in fridge for 10-30 minutes before continuing.
3. Preheat oven to 400°F. Line a baking sheet with parchment paper; set aside.
4. Carefully wrap 2-3 strips of zucchini around a chicken strip, covering as much of the chicken as possible. Place strip seam-side down on prepared baking sheet. Repeat with remaining zucchini and chicken.
5. Brush each piece well with remaining sauce. Roll up any extra zucchini strips and place them on the baking sheet as well.
6. Bake for about 20 minutes, until chicken is cooked through.

Plan Ahead These can be prepared a day or two ahead; reheat, loosely covered, until warmed through..

Veggie-Topped Confetti Chicken

Meat | Yield 4-6 servings

Many people want cutlets that aren't breaded or fried, so I'm happy to present this fabulous option. Inspired by my sister Sarah, this chicken gets flavor from the vegetables, which keep it juicy and make it look so pretty!

- **1½ cups** shredded carrots (about **2 medium** carrots)
- **1½ cups** shredded green cabbage
- **4-5** scallions, sliced
- **2 cloves** garlic, minced
- **1 cube** frozen ginger OR **1 teaspoon** ground ginger
- **1 Tablespoon** spicy brown mustard
- **1 teaspoon** soy sauce
- **1 Tablespoon** lime juice OR lemon juice
- **3 Tablespoons** olive oil
- **4-6** chicken cutlets
- olive oil, for drizzling
- kosher salt, for sprinkling
- black pepper, for sprinkling

1. Preheat oven to 375°F. Line baking sheet with parchment paper; set aside.
2. In a large bowl, combine carrots, cabbage, scallions, garlic, ginger, mustard, soy sauce, lime juice, and olive oil. Set aside.
3. Place chicken cutlets on prepared baking sheet. Drizzle olive oil over chicken; sprinkle with salt and pepper. Place vegetable mixture over the chicken cutlets, covering them fully.
4. Bake for about 30 minutes, until chicken is cooked through.

Plan Ahead These can be prepared a day or two ahead; reheat, loosely covered, until warmed through..

Honey Garlic Chicken Fingers

Meat | Yield 6-8 servings

My family, and many thousands of others, have made, enjoyed and raved about the pretzel-crusted chicken fingers recipe in my previous cookbook, ***Real Life Kosher Cooking****. Shabbos lunch in my home was never complete without them — until I came up with this version. An incredibly crispy, sweet and savory baked chicken finger that's packed with flavor. A new favorite has been born!*

2½ pounds chicken cutlets, cut into fingers

2 Tablespoons flour

1 egg

1 Tablespoon honey, plus more, for coating

½ cup garlic mayo, (see below)

2 cups cracker crumbs or flatbread crumbs (see Note)

GARLIC MAYO

1 cup mayonnaise

4 cubes frozen garlic

2 Tablespoons lemon juice

2-4 teaspoons sugar OR sweetener, optional

1. Preheat oven to 400°F. Line 2 baking sheets with parchment paper. Coat parchment well with oil or nonstick cooking spray; set aside.
2. In a large bowl, combine chicken pieces with flour. Toss until all chicken is fully coated.
3. **Prepare the garlic mayo:** In a small bowl combine all garlic mayo ingredients until smooth.
4. In a small bowl, stir together egg, honey, and ½ cup garlic mayo. Pour over floured chicken; stir until fully coated.
5. Place crumbs onto a wide, shallow dish. Press each chicken finger into crumbs to fully coat on all sides; place on prepared baking sheets. Do not place the fingers too close together on the baking sheets.
6. Before baking, spray the chicken fingers well with nonstick cooking spray; drizzle a thin stream of honey across the chicken. (Use more or less depending on how sweet you like it!)
7. Bake for 6 minutes, then flip and bake 6-7 minutes, until cooked through.
8. Serve hot, with remaining Garlic Mayo for dipping, optional.

Note You can use your favorite crackers to make crumbs, processing them until crushed, but with some texture remaining. You can save time by using panko crumbs, but my recommendation is to use garlic-flavored flatbread crackers for an amazing garlic flavor throughout!

Plan Ahead These chicken fingers freeze nicely. Defrost, then serve at room temperature or reheat, in a single layer, uncovered.

Sweet and Tangy Lemon Chicken Poppers

Meat | Yield 6-8 servings

Takeout fakeout! I don't fry chicken very often, so when I do, you know it's gotta be VERY worth it.

BATTER

1 cup flour

½ cup cornstarch

2 teaspoons kosher salt

½ teaspoon black pepper

2 teaspoons baking powder

2 eggs

1 cup seltzer OR water

CHICKEN

2½ pounds chicken cutlets, cut into bite-sized pieces

¼ cup flour

oil, for frying

LEMON SAUCE

zest of 1 lemon

½ cup freshly squeezed lemon juice (from 3-4 lemons)

¼ cup rice vinegar

⅔ cup sugar

¼ cup water

2 Tablespoons cornstarch, dissolved in 2 Tablespoons cold water

1 Tablespoon soy sauce

1. **Prepare the batter:** In a medium bowl, whisk together flour, cornstarch, salt, pepper, and baking powder until combined.
2. Add eggs and seltzer. Whisk until smooth and combined. Set aside.
3. **Prepare the chicken:** In a large bowl, toss chicken with flour until sticky. Add batter to bowl. Toss until all chicken is fully coated.
4. Heat 1½-2 inches of oil in a deep frying pan over medium-high heat.
5. Add chicken to hot oil; fry for 5-8 minutes, flipping halfway through, until chicken is cooked through. Work in batches to avoid overcrowding the pan. Remove chicken to paper towels to drain; set aside.
6. **Prepare the lemon sauce:** Bring lemon zest, lemon juice, vinegar, sugar, and water to a boil in a small pot. Add cornstarch mixture; simmer until sauce is slightly thickened. Remove from heat; stir in soy sauce.
7. Just before serving, toss chicken in lemon sauce in a large bowl to fully coat. Alternatively, serve chicken with the sauce on the side as a dip.

Variation In place of the lemon sauce, you can use your favorite bottled sauce, such as teriyaki or General Tso's sauce. Alternatively, omit the sauce for plain battered chicken.

Plan Ahead Although best when served freshly fried, chicken can be fried a few days ahead of time. Reheat, uncovered, in a single layer, until warmed through. Sauce can be prepared ahead of time and frozen until ready to use.

Spinach Chicken Burgers

Meat | Yield 4 large burgers

When I first made these, I have to admit I was a little surprised at just how good spinach and chicken could actually be! Pair them with portobello "buns" for a fantastically filling, healthy, full meal.

- **1 Tablespoon** olive oil
- **1 small** onion, diced
- **1½ teaspoon** kosher salt
- **6 cloves** garlic, minced
- **1 pound** frozen spinach, defrosted and squeezed dry
- **1 teaspoon** dried parsley
- **2 Tablespoons** red wine vinegar
- **1½ pounds** ground chicken, preferably dark
- **2** eggs
- **½ cup** breadcrumbs, regular OR whole wheat
- **1 teaspoon** kosher salt
- oil, for frying
- lettuce, for topping, optional
- sliced tomatoes, for topping, optional

1. Heat oil over medium heat in large frying pan. Add onion and salt. Cook 5-10 minutes, until onion has softened.
2. Add garlic, spinach, parsley, and vinegar. Cook on medium low for 10 minutes. Remove to a large bowl and set aside to cool.
3. Once cooled, add remaining ingredients; stir until evenly distributed.
4. Heat a large frying pan over high heat. Form patties of the chicken mixture; sear over high heat for 1-2 minutes per side to form a crust. Reduce heat; cook about 5 minutes, until fully cooked through. Serve on a portobello bun (see Note), if desired, and choice of toppings, such as lettuce or sliced tomatoes.

Note To make a portobello bun, as pictured, drizzle olive oil over mushroom caps; sprinkle with salt and pepper. Broil or grill portobellos on high for 6-7 minutes per side, until cooked through.

Plan Ahead Chicken mixture can be prepared and frozen raw, then defrosted and fried fresh.

Grilled Burger Wraps

Meat | Yield 4 servings

I love a good burger served the traditional way, but sometimes I find them hard to eat. My solution? The burger wrap! First, the super-thin wrap means more room for toppings, while still fitting it all into your mouth. But the best part is the way it forms a self-contained pouch, keeping the mess to a minimum and the flavor to a maximum!

CHILI GARLIC DIP

½ cup mayonnaise

4 cloves garlic, minced

1 teaspoon kosher salt

1½ teaspoons chili powder

1 Tablespoon honey

1 Tablespoon lemon juice OR lime juice

CARAMELIZED ONIONS

3 Tablespoons oil

2 large Spanish onions, sliced

1 teaspoon kosher salt

¼ teaspoon black pepper

1 Tablespoon sugar, optional

BURGERS

1½ pounds ground beef

kosher salt, to taste

black pepper, to taste

ASSEMBLY

4 wraps

1 large beefsteak tomato, sliced

2 pickles, sliced on the diagonal

1. **Prepare the chili garlic dip:** Combine all dip ingredients in a small bowl; stir until smooth. Set aside.
2. **Prepare the caramelized onions:** Heat oil in a large frying pan over medium heat. Add onions, salt, pepper, and sugar. Stir to combine.
3. Turn heat to low and cook, stirring occasionally, for 30-40 minutes, until the onions are golden brown and caramelized. Set aside.
4. **Prepare the burgers:** Divide meat into four 6-ounce portions. Shape each portion into a patty. For best results, use your thumb to create an indentation in the center, to promote even cooking of the burger. Season both sides of each patty well with salt and pepper.
5. Heat a grill pan or grill to medium-high heat. Add burgers; cook for 3-4 minutes, then flip and cook an additional 3-4 minutes, or until desired doneness is reached. Set aside.
6. **Assemble the wrap:** Spread a large spoonful of chili garlic dip in the center of a wrap. Top with a burger, a slice of tomato, some pickle slices, and some caramelized onions. Fold the wrap around the burger, forming a packet.
7. Place the packet, seam side down, into a hot grill pan or grill. Cook on high for about 1 minute, then flip and cook on the other side for 1 minute. Repeat with remaining burgers and wraps.

Note The toppings here are my suggestions, based on what I enjoy, but feel free to change it up based on your preferences. Just remember that whatever toppings you add will cook inside the wrap for 2 minutes, so avoid lettuce and the like, which won't hold up to the cooking.

Plan Ahead Chili Garlic Dip can be made up to a week ahead; Caramelized Onions can be made 2-3 days ahead. Burgers should be made and assmebled fresh.

Orange Sesame Kebabs

Meat | Yield 6-8 servings

Looking for a new, family-friendly way to use chopped meat? Look no further than these slightly sweet, super-flavorful, and totally easy kebabs!

SAUCE

½ cup fresh squeezed orange juice

¼ cup honey

2 Tablespoons soy sauce

1 Tablespoon toasted sesame oil

2 Tablespoons rice vinegar

2 Tablespoons sesame seeds

4 cloves garlic, minced

1 cube frozen ginger

1 teaspoon kosher salt

1 teaspoon onion powder

KEBABS

2 pounds ground beef

2 eggs

½ cup breadcrumbs

SPECIAL EQUIPMENT

6-8 large metal or wooden skewers (see Note)

1. Preheat oven to 350°F. Line a baking sheet with foil; coat well with nonstick cooking spray. Set aside.
2. **Prepare the sauce:** In a medium bowl, whisk together all sauce ingredients until combined. Set aside.
3. **Prepare the kebabs:** In large bowl, combine meat, eggs, breadcrumbs, and about ¾ of the sauce.
4. Form meat mixture around skewers to form kebab shapes, dividing it between 6-8 large skewers. Place on prepared baking sheet.
5. Brush half the remaining sauce over the kebabs, then roast for 25 minutes.
6. Carefully flip the kebabs; brush with remaining sauce. Set oven to broil; broil for about 4 minutes, until they start to caramelize.

Plan Ahead Kebabs can be baked up to 2 days ahead. Rewarm, uncovered, until heated through.

Note If using wooden skewers, prevent them from burning by soaking them in water for half an hour before forming the kebabs around them.

Barbecue Beef Lasagna

Meat | Yield 8 servings

I've been making variations of this barbecue beef recipe for the longest time, and it's always a requested favorite. It started out as beef pizza (see Variation), then it became beef calzones, and finally, I settled on this easy, weeknight version: barbecue beef lasagna.

MEAT MIXTURE

- **1 Tablespoon** oil
- **2 pounds** ground beef
- **1 teaspoon** kosher salt
- **½ teaspoon** black pepper

SAUCE

- **1 Tablespoon** oil
- **2 large** onions, diced
- **1 teaspoon** kosher salt
- **4 cloves** garlic, minced
- **1½ cups** barbecue sauce, homemade (page 286) or store bought

ASSEMBLY

- **¾ cup** mayonnaise
- **1 (1-pound) box** lasagna noodles
- **1 cup** water

1. In large frying pan over high heat, heat oil. Add meat, salt, and pepper; cook, stirring frequently to break up chunks, until meat is mostly browned, for a few minutes. Remove from pan; set aside.
2. **Prepare the sauce:** Lower heat to medium. To the same pan, add oil, onions, salt, and garlic. Cook for 5 minutes, until onions have softened.
3. Add barbecue sauce; raise heat to high and bring to a boil, then remove from heat. Pour of the mixture into the meat; reserve the remaining sauce.
4. **Assemble lasagna:** Preheat oven to 350°F. Mix mayonnaise into reserved sauce.
5. Spread a small amount of sauce into a 9x13-inch pan. Reserving most of the remaining sauce for the top layer, layer uncooked lasagna noodles, a thin layer of sauce, and meat mixture, finishing with noodles. Add a generous layer of sauce over the top layer of noodles; make sure to cover all the noodle surface so that the noodles will cook fully. Pour a cup of water into the pan.
6. Cover; bake for 40 minutes. Uncover; bake for 10 minutes.

Variation To make an easy and delicious BBQ Beef Pizza, spread sauce over a store-bought pizza dough, then top with meat mixture. Bake at 375°F until edges are crispy and meat is cooked through. Drizzle with garlic mayo (page 134) before serving.

Plan Ahead Lasagna can be prepared ahead and frozen until ready to use. Reheat, covered, at 350°F until warmed through.

Baked Meatballs in Asian Peanut Sauce

Meat | Yield 6-8 servings

If your family wants a change from the traditional meatballs you usually make, give this Asian-inspired version a try! The peanut sauce is super flavorful, and I made these completely in the oven, so there's no pot to wash.

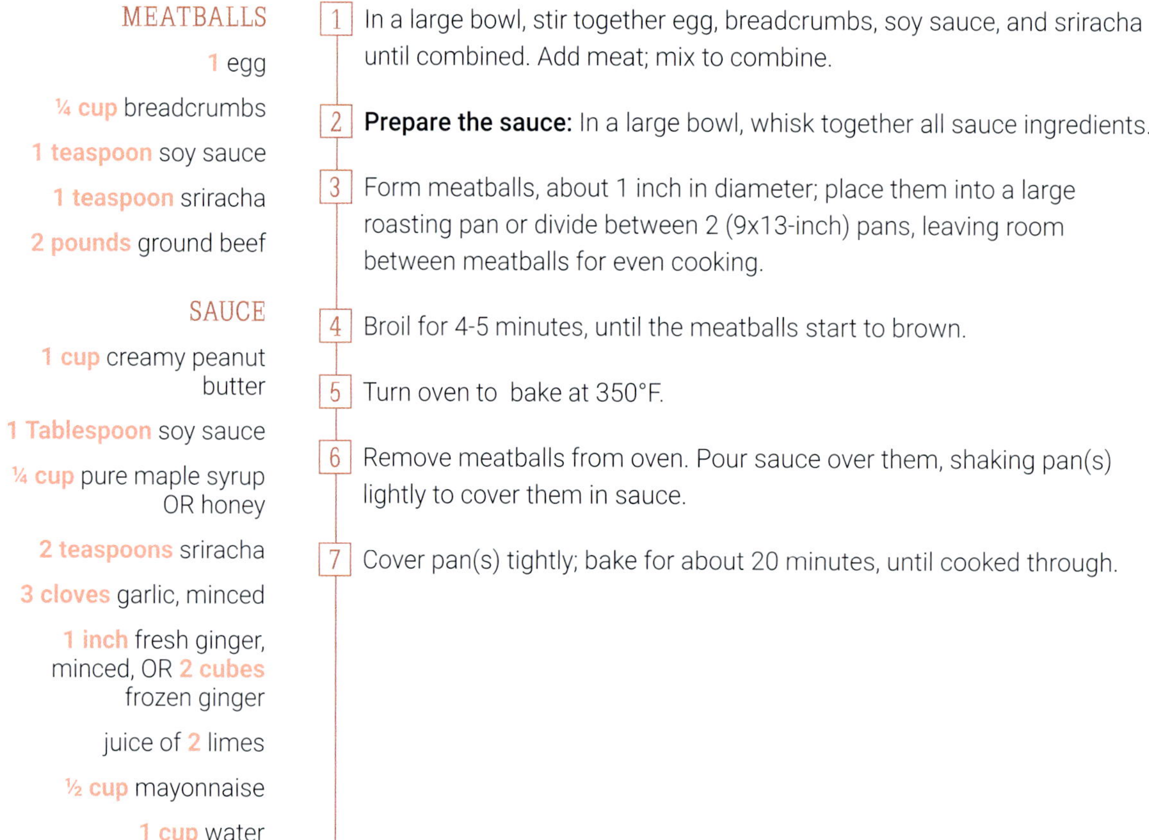

MEATBALLS

1 egg

¼ cup breadcrumbs

1 teaspoon soy sauce

1 teaspoon sriracha

2 pounds ground beef

SAUCE

1 cup creamy peanut butter

1 Tablespoon soy sauce

¼ cup pure maple syrup OR honey

2 teaspoons sriracha

3 cloves garlic, minced

1 inch fresh ginger, minced, OR 2 cubes frozen ginger

juice of 2 limes

½ cup mayonnaise

1 cup water

1. In a large bowl, stir together egg, breadcrumbs, soy sauce, and sriracha until combined. Add meat; mix to combine.
2. **Prepare the sauce:** In a large bowl, whisk together all sauce ingredients.
3. Form meatballs, about 1 inch in diameter; place them into a large roasting pan or divide between 2 (9x13-inch) pans, leaving room between meatballs for even cooking.
4. Broil for 4-5 minutes, until the meatballs start to brown.
5. Turn oven to bake at 350°F.
6. Remove meatballs from oven. Pour sauce over them, shaking pan(s) lightly to cover them in sauce.
7. Cover pan(s) tightly; bake for about 20 minutes, until cooked through.

Plan Ahead Meatballs can be prepared ahead of time and frozen in the sauce until ready to serve. Reheat, covered, until warmed through.

Crockpot Pineapple Pepper Steak

Meat | Yield 6 servings

People often ask me the secret to soft, melt-in-your mouth pepper steak, and the answer is simple: Cook it low and slow. Naturally, this makes it a great candidate for a crockpot meal. The pineapple tenderizes the meat and adds fantastic flavor, making a dish that's simple enough for a weeknight but nice enough for a Shabbos or holiday meal.

2-3 pounds pepper steak cut into small, thin strips

3 Tablespoons cornstarch

1 teaspoon kosher salt

oil, for frying

PINEAPPLE SAUCE

2 Tablespoons oil

2 red onions, diced

1 teaspoon kosher salt

4-6 cloves garlic, minced

1 red bell pepper, diced

1 green bell pepper, diced

⅓ cup honey

1 (15-ounce) can crushed pineapple, with its juice

¼ cup soy sauce

1 Tablespoon sriracha OR hot sauce

½ teaspoon ground ginger, optional

½ cup ketchup

sliced scallions, optional, for garnish

1. In a large bowl, toss together meat, cornstarch, and salt.
2. Heat a thin layer of oil in a large, deep frying pan over high heat. Working in batches to avoid overcrowding the pan, sear the meat for about 1 minute per side, until browned. Transfer meat to crockpot; no need to wash pan before continuing with the recipe.
3. **Prepare the sauce:** Using the same pan, lower heat to medium. Add oil, onions, salt, garlic, and peppers. Cook for about 5 minutes, until softened.
4. Add remaining sauce ingredients; raise heat and bring mixture to a boil. Pour sauce over meat in crockpot, stir, and cook on low for 6-8 hours or on high for about 4 hours.

Variation For an oven version of this dish, after sautéing the meat, add meat and sauce ingredients to a 9x13 pan. Cover tightly; bake at 325°F for about 2 hours, until meat is tender.

Plan Ahead This dish can be prepared ahead and frozen until ready to serve. For best results, prepare meat using the oven variation before freezing.

Roasted Mushroom Minute Steak

Meat | Yield 6-8 servings

This fabulous minute steak couldn't be simpler to make, but the flavor is extraordinary. This recipe has no sugar, wine, or unhealthy ingredients — just another reason to love this dish!

2 (8-10-ounce) boxes white mushrooms, sliced

2 (8-10-ounce) boxes baby bella mushrooms, sliced

¼ cup olive oil

1½ teaspoons kosher salt

¼ teaspoon black pepper

4 cloves garlic, minced OR **4 cubes** frozen garlic

2-3 pounds minute steak

kosher salt, to taste

black pepper, to taste

1. Preheat oven to 350°F.
2. Place mushrooms, oil, salt, pepper, and garlic into a large bowl. Toss to combine.
3. Divide mushroom mixture between 2 (9x13-inch) pans. Roast, uncovered, for 35 minutes.
4. Meanwhile, sprinkle salt and pepper over both sides of the minute steaks. After 35 minutes, add steaks to roasting pans, covering them with roasted mushrooms.
5. Cover pans tightly and bake for 2-2½ hours, until meat is fork-tender.

Variation You can make this fresh on Yom Tov, even if your oven isn't on. Sauté the mushrooms in a deep frying pan, then bury the steaks under them. Cover; simmer over low heat until the meat is softened. You may need to add a cup or two of liquid, such as chicken broth or red wine, to keep it from sticking.

Plan Ahead This dish can be cooked and frozen until ready to serve. Reheat, covered, until warmed through.

Sweet and Sour Cabbage Braised Flanken

Meat | Yield 6 servings

I was inspired by traditional meat and cabbage soup, with its sweet and sour flavors, and came up with a main dish version. If you enjoy meat that's both flavorful and so tender it's falling off the bone, this is definitely the dish for you!

- **3 pounds** bone-in flanken
- kosher salt, for sprinkling
- black pepper, for sprinkling
- **2 Tablespoons** oil
- **1** onion, sliced
- **1½ teaspoons** kosher salt, divided
- **1 pound** shredded green cabbage
- **1 teaspoon** garlic powder
- juice of **2** lemons
- **¼ cup** sugar
- **1 (6-ounce) can** tomato paste
- **½ cup** water

1. Preheat oven to 300°F.
2. Sprinkle salt and pepper all over both sides of meat. Sear meat in a large, hot frying pan for about 2 minutes per side, until browned. No need to wash frying pan before continuing with the recipe. Transfer flanken into a large roasting pan.
3. Add oil, onion, and ¾ teaspoon salt to the frying pan. Sauté for about 5 minutes, until softened.
4. Add cabbage and garlic. Cook for an additional 5 minutes. Add lemon juice, sugar, tomato paste, and remaining ¾ teaspoon salt. Stir to combine. Pour cabbage mixture over flanken in roasting pan. Pour ½ cup of water over cabbage mixture.
5. Cover pan tightly; bake for 3½-4 hours, until the meat is very tender and falling off the bone.

Plan Ahead This dish can be prepared ahead and frozen. Rewarm, fully covered, until warmed through.

Matbucha Brisket

Meat | Yield 6-8 servings

I frequently get requests for non-sweet roast recipes, and I love to fulfill that request because my family prefers their Yom Tov roasts savory too, and I'm always looking for the next great idea. This one stuck me one day when I thought about matbucha — the ever-popular dip made from vegetables. I decided to braise a roast in a matbucha-inspired sauce, and the meat was so incredibly flavorful, I knew it was a winner!

- **1 (about 3-pound)** second cut brisket (see Note)
- kosher salt, for sprinkling
- black pepper, for sprinkling.
- **3 Tablespoons** oil
- **2** onions, sliced
- **2 teaspoons** kosher salt, divided
- **3** bell peppers, sliced, preferably different colors
- **2** plum tomatoes, diced
- **5 cloves** garlic, minced
- **½** jalapeño pepper, minced
- **2 teaspoons** cumin
- **1 teaspoon** chili powder
- **1 (28-ounce) can** diced tomatoes

1. Preheat oven to 325°F. Sprinkle salt and pepper over both sides of roast.
2. Heat a large, deep frying pan over high heat. Add roast; sear for 2-3 minutes per side, until browned on the outside. Transfer to a roasting pan; set aside.
3. Turn heat under the frying pan to medium; add oil, onions, and 1 teaspoon salt. Cook for about 5 minutes, until softened
4. Add peppers, tomatoes, garlic, jalapeño, and remaining teaspoon salt. Cook for 8-10 minutes, until softened.
5. Raise heat to high. Add cumin, chili powder, and diced tomatoes with their liquid. Cook until mixture starts to bubble around the edges. Pour vegetable mixture over the meat.
6. Cover roasting pan tightly; bake for 40-50 minutes per pound, until meat is soft and tender.

Note Instead of a brisket, you can use french roast, minute roast, or any other cut of meat that does well when cooked low and slow.

Plan Ahead This meat freezes well in the sauce, wrapped and airtight. Reheat, covered, until warmed through.

Overnight Bourbon Barbecue Ribs

Meat | Yield 5 servings

I'm proud to say that this recipe has evolved over the 7 years since I originally created it. I used my increased food knowledge and tidbits I picked up from chefs I know to transform the dish. Instead of braising the meat for the full 6-8 hours in barbecue sauce, which yields a very heavy meat, I learned to braise it in a lighter broth-like liquid, then add the sauce at the end — plenty of time to give the meat flavor without adding the heaviness.

3 pounds spare ribs or short ribs

oil, for searing

kosher salt, for sprinkling

black pepper, for sprinkling

2 onions, sliced

4 cloves garlic, chopped

1½ teaspoons kosher salt

½ teaspoon black pepper

1 cup chicken broth OR water

1 cup Bourbon Barbecue Sauce (page 286)

1. Preheat oven to 250°F.
2. Heat oil in a large frying pan over high heat. Sprinkle salt and pepper over all sides of the ribs. Sear for a minute or two per side, until browned. Transfer to a large roasting pan.
3. Add onions, garlic, salt, and pepper to roasting pan. Add broth.
4. Cover pan tightly; bake overnight (or about 6-8 hours), until tender. Remove onions from pan and brush barbecue sauce generously over each rib. Return to oven and bake, covered, for an additional hour.
5. Raise oven temperature to 400°F. Uncover pan; bake for about 10 minutes, until sauce is caramelized.

Plan Ahead The ribs can be frozen, well wrapped, until ready to serve. Rewarm, tightly covered, until heated through.

Red Wine and Shallot Glazed Corned Beef

Meat | Yield 6-8 servings

Often people think of corned beef as topped with a super-sweet, heavy glaze, but this one is different. It's bursting with flavor, not too sweet. It's no wonder this was such an instant hit at a large party I hosted — and the corned beef was polished off almost immediately!

1 (3-4-pound) pickled corned beef deckle OR 2nd cut corned beef brisket

GLAZE

1 Tablespoon oil

2-3 shallots, finely diced

1 teaspoon kosher salt

2 cloves garlic, minced

¾ cup red wine (I used semi-sweet)

¼ cup balsamic vinegar

⅓ cup honey

1. Preheat oven to 350°F.
2. Place corned beef, along with pickling liquid from the bag, into a large roasting pan. Fill pan with water covering the meat fully. Cover pan tightly and place in oven.
3. Bake for about 3 hours, until meat is fork tender. Set aside to cool.
4. **Prepare the glaze:** Heat oil in a small pot over medium heat. Add shallots, salt, and garlic; sauté for about 10 minutes, until shallots have softened and start to get some color.
5. Add wine, vinegar, and honey. Raise heat; bring mixture to a boil. Reduce heat; simmer for 20-30 minutes, until mixture has thickened. Use an immersion blender, blender, or food processor to puree mixture until completely smooth and thickened.
6. Once meat has cooled, slice thinly; pour sauce over sliced beef.
7. Preheat oven to 375°F. Bake, uncovered, for 15-20 minutes.

Plan Ahead This meat can be prepared a day or two ahead of time. Slice it after it has cooled; reheat, loosely covered, until warmed through.

Raspberry Honey Mustard Silver Tip Roast

Meat | Yield 6 servings

Have you ever wandered through the aisles of a gourmet food store, looking desperately for a hechsher on various cool and delicious-looking products? That's me, every time. On one such occasion, after looking and looking for a hechsher on a raspberry honey mustard spread (I didn't find one), I realized that I could make my own. And I did. And it became the perfect sauce for a delicious roast.

2 onions, sliced

1 (3-pound) silver tip roast

RASPBERRY HONEY MUSTARD SAUCE

½ cup raspberry jam

½ cup Dijon mustard

2 Tablespoons honey

2 teaspoons hot sauce

1 teaspoon kosher salt

2 cloves garlic, minced

1 teaspoon soy sauce

1 Tablespoon olive oil

1. **Prepare the sauce:** In a small bowl, whisk together all sauce ingredients.
2. **Prepare the roast:** Place sliced onions into a roasting pan; toss together with half the sauce mixture. Rub remaining sauce onto all sides of roast; place into pan. For best results, let meat marinate in the sauce for about 30 minutes, allowing flavors to combine.
3. Preheat oven to 450°F.
4. Roast meat, uncovered, for 10 minutes. Reduce oven temperature to 350°F. Cover meat; bake for 70-90 minutes, depending on size of roast, until it reaches desired level of doneness. For best results, check internal temperature with a meat thermometer. Cook meat to about 130°F, which is medium rare. (The meat will continue to cook after it's removed from the oven, bringing it to medium.)
5. Allow meat to rest for 10-15 minutes before slicing.

Plan Ahead Meat can be prepared a day or two ahead. If reheating, undercook meat by a few degrees to ensure that it doesn't overcook while reheating.

Roasted Garlic Strip Steak

Meat | Yield 6 servings

Roasting garlic turns the usually sharp and savory flavors into a sweet and intense flavor that works so perfectly with the meat. When roasting the garlic, you may want to make a few extra — the soft and buttery roasted cloves are a wonderful accompaniment to the steak!

2-3 (1-pound each) strip steaks

ROASTED GARLIC

3 heads garlic

2 Tablespoons olive oil

1 teaspoon kosher salt

½ teaspoon black pepper

RUB

1 Tablespoon olive oil

1 teaspoon red wine vinegar

1 teaspoon soy sauce

1 teaspoon honey

1. **Prepare the roasted garlic:** Preheat oven to 400°F. Set out a baking sheet.
2. Cut the tops from each head of garlic, revealing the cloves inside. Discard the tops; place each head on a piece of foil large enough to enclose it.
3. Drizzle oil, salt, and pepper over the garlic. Fold the foil around the garlic, enclosing it completely.
4. Place foil-wrapped garlic onto prepared pan (in case of any leakage); bake for 40-50 minutes, until garlic is golden brown. Set aside to cool before continuing.
5. **Prepare the rub:** Squeeze the garlic onto a cutting board to extract all cloves. Discard the peel.
6. Use the back of a knife to mash the garlic. Transfer garlic to a bowl; add rub ingredients. Mix to make a paste.
7. Smear garlic rub all over every side of the meat. Cover meat; marinate in the fridge for 1-2 hours, up to overnight.
8. Preheat oven to 350°F. Heat a grill pan over high heat. Add steaks; sear for 1 minute per side. Place into a 9x13-inch pan.
9. Depending on the thickness of the meat, bake for 15-20 minutes, turning meat every 5 minutes, until it reaches desired level of doneness. For best results, use a meat thermometer. The center of the meat should be about 130°F for medium rare.
10. Let steak rest for 10-15 minutes before slicing.

Plan Ahead Prepare roasted garlic rub and rub all over steak, then freeze until ready to cook. ■ If you plan to rewarm the cooked steak, undercook it so it doesn't become too well done when you reheat it.

Thai Marinated London Broil

Meat | Yield 6-8 servings

This recipe has been a fan favorite on my food blog for years, since I initially published the recipe. People rave about how easy it is, how flavorful it is, and most importantly, how it uses pantry staple ingredients!

1 (approx. 2-pound) London broil

MARINADE

2 Tablespoons lime juice

⅓ cup rice vinegar

1 Tablespoon toasted sesame oil

¼ cup canola oil

¼ cup soy sauce

2 Tablespoons honey

2 cloves garlic, minced OR **2 cubes** frozen garlic

½ teaspoon ground ginger

2 scallions, thinly sliced (optional)

1. Combine all marinade ingredients in a small bowl. Whisk to combine. Pour over meat.
2. Cover and refrigerate for a few hours, up to overnight.
3. If desired, sprinkle sliced scallions over the meat before broiling.
4. Place the meat and marinade in a 9x13-inch pan. Broil on high for 7 minutes. Turn meat over; broil 6-8 minutes, depending on the thickness of the meat and your desired level of doneness. For best results, use a meat thermometer to ensure you cook your meat to the correct temperature. I like to serve it medium rare, which is when the internal temperature of the meat is about 130°F.
5. Let meat rest for about 10 minutes before slicing.

Plan Ahead To reheat: Save the liquid after broiling the meat, and reheat in the same liquid. For best results, undercook the meat when cooking it initially, so it doesn't become overcooked when reheating.

GRAPEFRUIT AND SHALLOT ROASTED SALMON, PAGE 190

MAC AND CHEESE WAFFLES, PAGE 168

CHICKPEA BEET BURGERS, PAGE 182

ORANGE-GLAZED FLOUNDER, PAGE 188

ONE-POT CHEESY SPINACH PASTA, PAGE 170

SWEET PEA AND RICOTTA RAVIOLI IN BROWN BUTTER SAUCE, PAGE 174

Dairy *and* Meatless Mains

Mac and Cheese Waffles

Dairy | Yield 6-8 servings

This recipe is dedicated to all of my fellow "crispy bits" lovers who find themselves picking at the browned and crispy corners of everything, because they're obviously the best part. I finally came up with a way to ensure that every bite of deliciously cheesy mac and cheese is as crispy and browned as those prized bits: a waffle iron!

1 (1-pound) box elbow macaroni, cooked according to package directions

3 cups milk

3 Tablespoons flour

2 teaspoons kosher salt

½ teaspoon black pepper

1 teaspoon garlic powder

1 teaspoon onion powder

8 ounces shredded mozzarella cheese

8 ounces shredded cheddar cheese

2 cups panko bread crumbs

marinara sauce, for serving, optional

1. Combine milk and flour in a large pot over medium heat. Whisk to break up any lumps; cook for a few minutes, stirring occasionally, until mixture starts to bubble and thicken.
2. Add salt, pepper, garlic powder, and onion powder. Whisk to combine.
3. Reserve ½ cup of each cheese; add remaining cheese into the pot. Whisk to incorporate. Cook until cheese is completely melted. Stir in pasta; remove from heat.
4. Stir breadcrumbs into pasta mixture. Spread a layer of mixture over a heated waffle maker, then sprinkle reserved cheese over the top. Cook until waffles are crispy and browned on the outside; this will take longer than making traditional waffles, so be patient.

2 Serve with marinara sauce as a dipping sauce, if desired.

Variation If you don't have a waffle iron, you can make these as patties instead. Fry in a small amount of oil in a frying pan on medium heat for a couple of minutes per side, until golden brown and crispy.

Plan Ahead Prepare mixture through Step 3; then complete the final step just before serving. Alternatively, you can make the waffles fully; then reheat in the oven, in a single layer, uncovered, until warmed through.

One-Pot Cheesy Spinach Pasta

Dairy | Yield 6 servings

When you can boil your pasta, cook your veggies, and make a cheesy and delicious pasta dish all in one pot, you know you've got a real winner recipe!

1 stick (8 Tablespoons) butter, divided

1 Spanish onion, finely diced

3 cloves garlic, minced

1 Tablespoon kosher salt, divided

½ teaspoon black pepper

2 pounds frozen chopped spinach, defrosted and drained

4 cups milk

1½ cups water

1 pound pasta, such as rotini

2 cups shredded mozzarella cheese

blistered cherry or grape tomatoes, optional, for serving (see Note)

1. Melt half the butter in a large pot over medium heat.
2. Add onion, garlic, half the salt, and pepper. Sauté, stirring occasionally, until softened, 5-7 minutes.
3. Add spinach and remaining butter. Cook for 8-10 minutes.
4. Add milk, water, and remaining salt. Bring to a boil. Add pasta; simmer for 10-12 minutes, until pasta is cooked. Stir in cheese; cook until cheese is melted. If desired, serve with blistered cherry tomatoes.

Note To prepare blistered cherry tomatoes, toss 1 cup cherry or grape tomatoes with 1 tablespoon oil. Broil for 5-8 minutes, until starting to blacken.

Plan Ahead While best fresh, pasta can be prepared a day or two ahead of time. Rewarm in a pot, stirring often, until heated through.

Caramelized Onion and Cheese Manicotti

Dairy | Yield 6-8 servings

I sent this updated take on a classic dish over to a friend for supper one night, and she texted me later, gushing: Everyone from her meat-and-potatoes husband down to her pickiest kids enjoyed it!

CARAMELIZED ONIONS

2 Tablespoons oil

3 large onions, diced

1 teaspoon kosher salt

¼ teaspoon black pepper

2 teaspoons brown sugar

FILLING

1 (16-ounce) container cottage cheese (full fat)

4 ounces shredded mozzarella

1 egg

1 teaspoon kosher salt

1 teaspoon dried parsley

pinch cayenne pepper

ASSEMBLY

1 (8-ounce) box manicotti, cooked according to package directions

1-1½ cups marinara sauce

4 ounces shredded mozzarella

1. **Prepare the caramelized onions:** Heat oil over medium-low heat in a large frying pan. Add onions, salt, pepper, and sugar. Stir to combine. Sauté, stirring occasionally, for about 20 minutes. For best flavor, turn heat to low and cook for up to an hour. Set aside to cool.
2. **Prepare the filling:** In a large bowl, combine cheeses, egg, spices, and cooled onions.
3. Preheat oven to 350°F. Coat a 9x13-inch baking pan with nonstick cooking spray; set aside.
4. Fill cooked manicotti with cheese mixture (this is easiest to do with a piping bag); place into prepared baking pan.
5. Spread marinara sauce over the filled manicotti; sprinkle with cheese. Bake for about 40 minutes, until the cheese is bubbling and golden.

Plan Ahead You can prepare the filling and fill the manicotti a day or two ahead of time, then bake just before serving.

Sweet Pea and Ricotta Ravioli in Brown Butter Sauce

Dairy | Yield 8 servings

Homemade ravioli, made from scratch, is a complicated and time-consuming dish. But my shortcut — wonton wrappers — allows you to enjoy this delicious, elevated dish, without spending forever rolling out homemade pasta dough!

RAVIOLI

1 pound frozen peas

2 Tablespoons olive oil

3 cloves garlic, minced

2 cubes frozen basil

1 teaspoon kosher salt

½ teaspoon black pepper

1 (16-ounce) container ricotta cheese

2 (9-ounce) packages wonton wrappers

BROWNED BUTTER SAUCE

1 stick (½ cup) butter

kosher salt, to taste

black pepper, to taste

grated Parmesan cheese, for sprinkling, optional

1. **Prepare the ravioli:** Place peas into a pot of salted, boiling water. Cook for 2-3 minutes, until bright green. Drain, then immediately place peas into ice water to shock, stopping the cooking. Once peas have cooled, drain again; reserve ½ cup peas. Add remaining peas to the bowl of a food processor fitted with the "S" blade.

2. Add oil, garlic, basil, salt, and pepper. Process until peas are smooth. Transfer mixture to a large bowl. Add ricotta cheese; stir to combine.

3. Place about 1 tablespoon mixture onto the center of a wonton wrapper, then rub water around the entire edge. Fold wrapper in half; press well to seal. Repeat with remaining wrappers and cheese mixture.

4. Heat a large pot of salted water over high heat. Add a splash of oil. Boil the ravioli for 5 minutes, working in batches to avoid overcrowding the pot. Drain and set aside, not touching one another, on a parchment-lined baking sheet.

5. **Prepare the sauce:** Heat a large frying pan over medium heat. Add butter; cook, swirling pan occasionally, for 3-4 minutes, until butter has melted and turned golden in color. Watch the butter carefully, as it will go from golden to burned very quickly.

6. Remove pan from heat. Add cooked ravioli and reserved peas. Sprinkle with salt, pepper,, and Parmesan cheese, if using. Stir to fully coat; serve immediately.

Plan Ahead Raviolis can be prepared ahead and frozen, raw. Boil fresh, then prepare sauce just before serving.

Cheese-Filled Veggie Ribbons

Dairy | Yield 4-6 Servings

Looking for a low-carb dairy option? These swirls of cheesy goodness are bound to fit the bill!

1 medium eggplant, thinly sliced into long strips

1 large zucchini, thinly sliced into long strips

1 large yellow squash, thinly sliced into long strips

2 Tablespoons olive oil

1 teaspoon kosher salt

CHEESE FILLING

1 (16-ounce) container low-fat cottage cheese

1 egg

1 cup shredded mozzarella cheese

¼ cup pesto (page 292, or store-bought)

ASSEMBLY

1 cup tomato sauce

½ cup mozzarella cheese, for sprinkling

1. Preheat oven to 400°F. Line 2 baking sheets with parchment paper.
2. Spread eggplant on 1 baking sheet; spread zucchini and yellow squash on second baking sheet. Toss vegetables on each baking sheet with 1 tablespoon oil and ½ teaspoon salt. The vegetables may overlap somewhat. Roast vegetables for 20 minutes. Set aside until cool enough to handle.
3. Preheat oven to 350°F. Spread tomato sauce into a 9-inch round pan.
4. **Prepare the cheese filling:** Combine all filling ingredients in a medium bowl. Working with one vegetable strip at a time, spread with a thin layer of filling and roll it up. Place into prepared pan (see photo). Repeat with remaining vegetables and filling.
5. Sprinkle ½ cup mozzarella cheese over filled veggie ribbons. Cover pan; bake for 20 minutes. Uncover pan; raise oven temperature to 400°F; bake for 20-30 minutes, until cheese is starting to brown.

Plan Ahead This dish can be prepared ahead and reheated a day or two later.

Mediterranean Panini

Dairy | Yield 4 servings

This dish is inspired by my sister Chaya and her friend Leah, who invited me to join them at a restaurant. Leah custom-ordered a calzone full of delicious Greek- and Mediterranean-inspired ingredients. I had the idea to make it a little simpler by using a panini press, and this dish was born.

GRILLED VEGETABLES

1 small eggplant, cut into sticks

1 large red bell pepper, sliced

1 medium Spanish onion, sliced

1 teaspoon kosher salt

½ teaspoon black pepper

2 Tablespoons olive oil

2 teaspoons balsamic vinegar

2 cloves garlic, minced

ASSEMBLY

4 baguettes, halved OR **8 slices** bread

mayonnaise, for spreading

4 ounces feta cheese, crumbled

1 cup shredded mozzarella cheese

12 sun-dried tomatoes, sliced

½ cup sliced black olives

1. Preheat panini press or sandwich maker.
2. Place vegetables into a bowl. Toss with salt, pepper, olive oil, vinegar, and garlic.
3. Lightly grease panini press; add about ¼ of the vegetable mixture. Grill for 5-6 minutes, until softened and vegetables have some grill lines. Remove from machine; repeat three more times with remaining vegetables. Set aside.
4. **Assemble panini:** Spread mayonnaise on each baguette half. On 4 of the baguette halves, layer ¼ of the mozzarella and feta cheeses; top with grilled vegetables, sun-dried tomatoes, and olives. Top with second half of each baguettes.
5. Place in panini press; grill for 5-6 minutes, or until cooked to desired level of doneness, depending on your machine.

Plan Ahead Vegetables can be grilled a day or two ahead of time. Sandwiches should be assembled fresh.

Hearty Vegetarian Chili

Pareve | Yield 8 servings

I originally created this chili recipe during the Nine Days, because as someone who doesn't eat much fish or dairy, I struggled with limited options. This dish is hearty and healthy – you won't miss the meat!

- **2 Tablespoons** oil
- **1 large** onion, diced
- **3 cloves** garlic, minced
- **2 teaspoons** kosher salt, divided
- ½ jalapeño pepper, finely chopped, or more, to taste (seeds and membrane removed)
- **1** red bell pepper, diced
- **1** carrot, shredded
- **1 small** butternut squash, diced
- **1 (15.5-ounce) can** red kidney beans
- **1 (15.5-ounce) can** black beans
- **1 (15.5-ounce) can** chickpeas
- **1 (14.5-ounce) can** diced tomatoes (preferably fire-roasted)
- **1 (15.5-ounce) can** tomato sauce
- **1 (6-ounce) can** tomato paste
- **1½ teaspoons** oregano
- **2 teaspoons** chili powder
- **1½ teaspoons** smoked paprika
- **1 teaspoon** cumin
- **2-2½ cups** water, to cover

1. Drain and rinse beans and chickpeas; set aside.
2. Heat oil in a large pot over medium heat. Add onion and 1 teaspoon salt; sauté, stirring occasionally, until onion is softened, 5-7 minutes.
3. Add garlic, jalapeño, red pepper, and carrot. Stir to combine; cook 10-15 minutes, until soft and fragrant.
4. Add butternut squash, all the beans, chickpeas, diced tomatoes, tomato sauce, tomato paste, remaining teaspoon salt and spices. Add water to cover.
5. Bring to a boil, then reduce heat and simmer for about 2 hours, until cooked through and fragrant.

Plan Ahead Chili can be cooked ahead and frozen in an airtight container. Reheat, covered, until warmed through.

Chickpea Beet Burgers

Pareve | Yield 8 servings

These burgers have a beautiful red color, thanks to the beets, and a ton of flavor that will have your family going back for doubles.

BURGERS

2 (15-ounce) cans chickpeas, drained and rinsed, divided

9 ounces cooked beets (see Note)

2 eggs

½ cup whole wheat flour

2 teaspoons kosher salt

2 teaspoons cumin

1 Tablespoon dried parsley

2 cloves garlic

1 teaspoon onion powder

1 teaspoon chili powder

1 teaspoon baking powder

oil, for pan-frying

ASSEMBLY

8 buns

hummus (page 50), or store-bought

sliced tomatoes, optional

Israeli pickles, optional

1. Place chickpeas from 1 can, beets, eggs, flour, salt, cumin, parsley, onion powder, chili powder, and baking powder into the bowl of a food processor fitted with the "S" blade. Process until mixture is completely smooth.
2. Add chickpeas from the second can; pulse in a few short bursts to break them up, but still leave some texture.
3. Heat a small amount of oil in a frying pan over medium-low heat. Form ½-cup burger mixture into a patty. Add to oil. Repeat with remaining mixture, working in batches so as not to overcrowd the pan.
4. Fry for about 5 minutes, until burgers are set. Flip and fry for another 3 minutes, until cooked through.
5. To serve, spread hummus on buns. Top with burgers and your choice of toppings, such as tomatoes or Israeli pickles.

Note For best results, use vacuum-packed cooked beets sold in packages. If they are not available, use canned beets.

Variation While the fried version is definitely better, you can prepare these in the oven as well. Bake at 400°F for about 15 minutes, flipping halfway through.

Plan Ahead The burgers can be prepared a day or two ahead and rewarmed, uncovered, until heated through. Assemble fresh.

Tofu Lo Mein

Pareve | Yield 6 servings

Many people are skeptical of tofu, but when it's prepared properly, tofu can be seriously delicious. This lo mein is packed with flavor and has turned many skeptics into fans.

2 (14-ounce) packages firm tofu

1 (1-pound) package lo mein noodles OR spaghetti

MARINADE

2 Tablespoons soy sauce

1 Tablespoon rice vinegar

½ teaspoon toasted sesame oil

1 teaspoon kosher salt

2 Tablespoons brown sugar

2 Tablespoons cornstarch

STIR FRY

2 Tablespoons oil, divided

1 large onion, diced

1 teaspoon kosher salt

1 (8-12-ounce) box white mushrooms, sliced

4 cloves garlic, minced

1 carrot, julienned

12 ounces broccoli

1 (14-ounce) can cut baby corn

SAUCE

¼ cup soy sauce

¼ cup honey

2 Tablespoons rice vinegar

1 Tablespoon toasted sesame oil

1. Wrap tofu in a clean towel and place a heavy pot or other heavy item over it. For best results, let sit for 1-2 hours to press out as much liquid as possible. Remove towel; cut tofu into thin slices.
2. **Prepare the noodles:** Cook noodles according to package directions. Drain, rinse, and set aside.
3. **Prepare the marinade:** In a large bowl, whisk together all marinade ingredients. Add tofu slices; marinate for at least 10 minutes, preferably up to 30 minutes.
4. **Prepare the stir fry:** In a large, deep frying pan or wok, heat 1 tablespoon oil over high heat. Add tofu to pan, discarding marinade. Sauté tofu, stirring often, for 4-5 minutes, until starting to brown. Remove from pan; set aside.
5. Heat remaining 1 tablespoon oil in the same pan over medium heat. Add onion, salt, mushrooms, and garlic. Cook, stirring occasionally, for about 8 minutes, until softened.
6. Add carrot, broccoli, and baby corn. Cook on high for 2 minutes.
7. **Prepare the sauce:** In a small bowl, whisk together all sauce ingredients.
8. Turn heat to low; pour sauce over vegetable mixture in pan. Add tofu and cooked noodles. Stir to combine, then cook on low for 2-3 minutes, until tofu, noodles, and vegetables are fully coated in sauce.

Variation You can make this as a traditional chicken lo mein instead. Use strips of chicken instead of tofu. When you add it to the pan at the end, you may need to cook it an extra few minutes to ensure the chicken has cooked all the way through.

Plan Ahead This dish is best fresh, but it can be refrigerated for a day or two, then reheated, loosely covered, in the oven until warmed through. For best results, add pasta fresh just before serving.

Crispy Beer-Battered Fish Sandwich

Pareve | Yield 4-6 servings

When people ask me for a fleishig place to eat out in Lakewood, New Jersey, I always recommend Snaps, a fantastic place with the motto, "Not fast food – good food fast." And let me tell you, the food there sure is good! The first time I ate there, owner Yussi Weisz brought me a crispy chicken sandwich, and I begged and begged for his secret to the ridiculously crispy coating. Finally, here it is. Yussie's earth-shatteringly crispy sandwich recipe – with his fish twist.

BATTER

1 cup flour

1¼ cups cornstarch

1 teaspoon kosher salt

¼ teaspoon black pepper

pinch cayenne pepper

1 (12-ounce) bottle beer, preferably lager

FISH

4-6 tilapia fillets

oil, for frying

kosher salt, for sprinkling

½ cup flour

1. **Prepare the batter:** Combine flour, cornstarch, salt, pepper, and cayenne pepper in a large bowl. Add beer; whisk really well to combine. Set aside.
2. **Prepare the fish:** Heat about 2 inches of oil in a deep frying pan over medium heat.
3. Sprinkle salt over both sides of a fish fillet. Dredge in flour to fully coat, then dip into prepared batter and submerge completely. Repeat with remaining fillets.
4. Fry fillets over medium heat for 4-5 minutes, until fish is cooked through and crispy. Remove to a paper towel-lined tray.
5. **Prepare the tangy tartar sauce:** Place pickle chips into a tall container. Using an immersion blender, chop pickles finely. (This can also be done in a food processor fitted with the "S" blade.) Add remaining sauce ingredients. Stir well to combine. Set aside.
6. **Assemble sandwich:** Spread a thick layer of sauce on the top and bottom of buns. Layer fish, lettuce, and tomato on bottom of bun; cover with top of bun.

Plan Ahead For best results, fry fish up to a day ahead. Just before serving, fry again on high for a minute or two, to get a really great crisp on the outside. Sauce can be made 2-3 days ahead and stored in the fridge in a closed container. Assemble sandwich just before serving.

TANGY TARTAR SAUCE

½ cup pickle chips

1 cup mayonnaise

½ teaspoon dry minced garlic

1 cube frozen parsley

2 cubes frozen dill

juice of **1** lemon

½ teaspoon hot sauce OR sriracha

ASSEMBLY

4-6 buns OR rolls

1-2 large beefsteak tomatoes, sliced

romaine lettuce

Orange-Glazed Flounder

Pareve | Yield 4-6 servings

*I met Rivky Kleiman, author of **Simply Gourmet**, through the food world, as colleagues at Mishpacha Magazine. We both prefer recipes that are easy, doable, and exciting without being too exotic. Rivky offered to share a delicious fish recipe in my book. I'm honored to give you a taste of her incredible food here.*

4-6 flounder fillets

kosher salt, for sprinkling

black pepper, for sprinkling

ORANGE GLAZE

¼ cup sweet orange marmalade

1 Tablespoon apple cider vinegar

1 Tablespoon orange juice

1 Tablespoon teriyaki sauce

½ teaspoon garlic powder

1 teaspoon kosher salt

½ teaspoon black pepper

1. Preheat oven to 400°F. Line a baking sheet with parchment paper. Set aside.
2. **Prepare the glaze:** In a small bowl, whisk together all orange glaze ingredients until combined.
3. Place flounder fillets on prepared baking sheet. Sprinkle with salt and pepper.
4. Brush each fillet with glaze. Bake for about 12 minutes, until cooked through. Serve with roasted butternut squash and green beans, if desired (see Note).

Note Optional side dish: Line a baking sheet with parchment paper. Cube 1 small butternut squash; toss with 3 Tablespoons olive oil and 2 teaspoons kosher salt. Place on one side of prepared baking sheet. Toss 1 pound of trimmed green beans with 1 tablespoon of olive oil and a teaspoon of kosher salt. Place on second half of baking sheet. Roast at 400°F for about 40 minutes, until vegetables are cooked through. Serve alongside fish.

Variation This glaze is delicious on salmon as well. Increase baking time to about 15 minutes.

Grapefruit and Shallot Roasted Salmon

Pareve | Yield 8 servings

This show-stopping salmon dish will impress all of your guests with its beautiful appearance and amazing taste!

- **1 side (approximately 2 pounds)** salmon
- **3** shallots, finely chopped or minced
- **3 cloves** garlic, minced
- **¾ cup** fresh parsley, chopped finely
- **2 Tablespoons** Dijon mustard
- **1 teaspoon** kosher salt
- **¼ teaspoon** black pepper
- **½ cup** olive oil
- **1 Tablespoon** honey
- **2** grapefruits, peel on, thinly sliced

1. Preheat oven to 350°F. Line a baking sheet with parchment paper.
2. Place salmon on prepared baking sheet.
3. In a medium bowl, combine shallots, garlic, parsley, mustard, salt, pepper, olive oil, and honey. Stir to combine and form a thick paste.
4. Spread mixture over the top of the salmon, covering it completely. Top with grapefruit slices.
5. Bake for 20-25 minutes, until cooked through. For nicest presentation, turn oven to broil. Broil salmon for a few minutes, until the grapefruit slices darken and caramelize slightly.

Plan Ahead Salmon can be prepared a day or two ahead of time. Serve cold or at room temperature.

Crispy Sweet and Spicy Salmon

Pareve | Yield 4-6 servings

I created this recipe together with my sister Chaya, who helped me put together the sweet and spicy flavors of the marinade and the wonderful crunch of the panko breadcrumbs, yielding a delicious fish your family will love!

4-6 salmon fillets

1 cup panko breadcrumbs

MARINADE

¼ cup hot sauce

¼ cup pure maple syrup OR honey

¼ cup orange juice

4 cloves garlic, minced

1 teaspoon kosher salt

1 teaspoon soy sauce

1. **Prepare the marinade:** In a large bowl, whisk together hot sauce, maple syrup, orange juice, garlic, salt and soy sauce.
2. Add salmon slices; marinate in the fridge for about 1 hour.
3. Preheat oven to 425°F. Line a baking sheet with parchment paper.
4. Place panko breadcrumbs into a large dish. Remove a fillet from the marinade; coat in panko crumbs and place on prepared baking sheet. Repeat with remaining fish and crumbs.
5. Bake about 15 minutes, until cooked through.
6. Transfer remaining marinade to a small pot; bring it to a boil. Reduce heat; simmer and cook until reduced and thickened. Serve this sauce alongside the salmon or drizzle over fillets.

Plan Ahead Fish can be prepared a day ahead and rewarmed, uncovered, until heated through.

GARLIC AND PARSLEY ROASTED CARROTS, PAGE 204

CORNED BEEF-TOPPED SMASHED POTATOES, PAGE 214

GARLIC GINGER UDON NOODLES, PAGE 216

OVERNIGHT ONIONS, PAGE 206

SNOW PEAS WITH CARAMELIZED SHALLOTS, PAGE 200

TWO-INGREDIENT SIDES, PAGE 226

Vegetables *and* Sides

Roasted Cauliflower Poppers

Pareve | Yield 6 servings

I originally had the idea for this recipe when eating "cauliflower poppers" at a restaurant. While enjoying the crispy breaded, deep-fried veggies, tossed in a delicious sauce, I wondered if I could get similar satisfying results by roasting unbreaded cauliflower until crispy, saving lots of calories. I went home and tinkered with the ingredients, and soon I was serving what my tasters describe as "the best cauliflower I ever had."

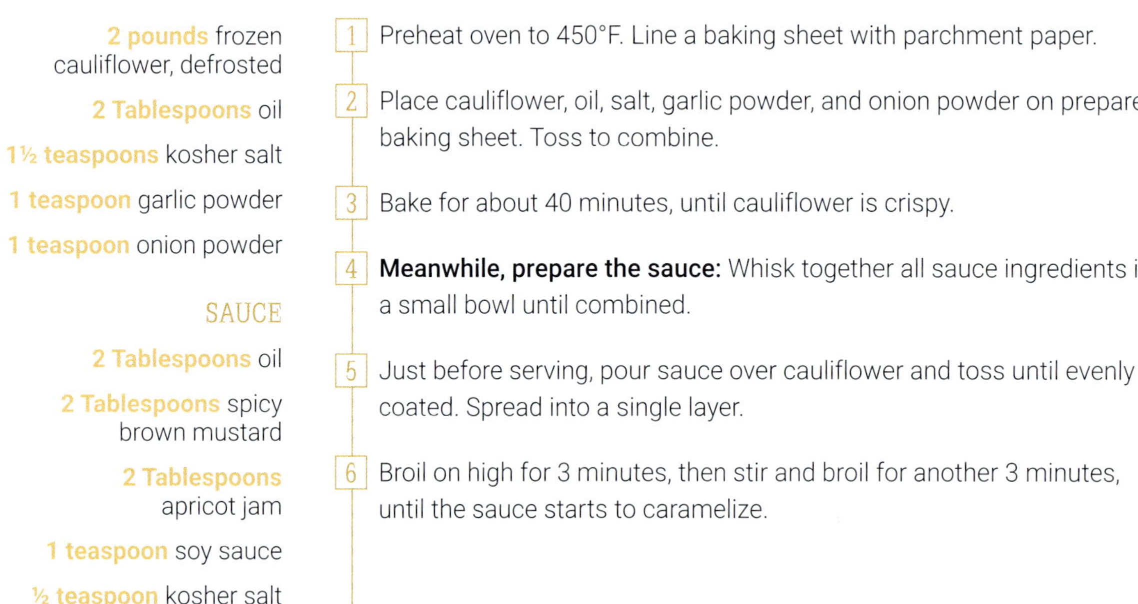

2 pounds frozen cauliflower, defrosted

2 Tablespoons oil

1½ teaspoons kosher salt

1 teaspoon garlic powder

1 teaspoon onion powder

SAUCE

2 Tablespoons oil

2 Tablespoons spicy brown mustard

2 Tablespoons apricot jam

1 teaspoon soy sauce

½ teaspoon kosher salt

1. Preheat oven to 450°F. Line a baking sheet with parchment paper.
2. Place cauliflower, oil, salt, garlic powder, and onion powder on prepared baking sheet. Toss to combine.
3. Bake for about 40 minutes, until cauliflower is crispy.
4. **Meanwhile, prepare the sauce:** Whisk together all sauce ingredients in a small bowl until combined.
5. Just before serving, pour sauce over cauliflower and toss until evenly coated. Spread into a single layer.
6. Broil on high for 3 minutes, then stir and broil for another 3 minutes, until the sauce starts to caramelize.

Plan Ahead Cauliflower can be roasted a day or two ahead. Sauce can be prepared ahead and stored in the fridge. For best results, toss sauce together with cauliflower and broil as close as possible to serving.

Variation To make this on the stovetop (such as for a Yom Tov meal), you can caramelize the cauliflower and sauce in a large frying pan, instead of using a broiler.

Herb-Roasted Green Beans

Pareve | Yield 6 servings

Sometimes you just need a basic, pull-some-staples-out-of-your-pantry, super-easy side dish. This is the one you'll find yourself making again and again.

- **3 Tablespoons** olive oil
- **1½ teaspoons** kosher salt
- **1½ teaspoons** dried basil
- **1½ teaspoons** dried oregano
- **1 Tablespoon** dried parsley
- **2 teaspoons** garlic powder
- **1 Tablespoon** balsamic vinegar
- **2 pounds** green beans, ends trimmed

1. Preheat oven to 425°F. Line a baking sheet with parchment paper; set aside.
2. In a small bowl, stir together oil, salt, basil, oregano, parsley, garlic, and red wine vinegar.
3. Place green beans on prepared baking sheet; toss with herb mixture to fully coat all green beans.
4. Bake for 30-35 minutes, until slightly shriveled.

Plan Ahead These green beans are best enjoyed fresh. They can be prepared a day or two ahead and enjoyed at room temperature. For best results, do not reheat.

Snow Peas
with Caramelized Shallots

Pareve | Yield 4-6 servings

I love snow peas when they're barely cooked and still really crunchy, but I wanted that amazing, slow-cooked flavor. My solution: Caramelize the shallots and develop a ton of flavor in them, then use that almost as a dressing, to coat the crispy snow peas. The result is simply fantastic.

2 Tablespoons olive oil

5 large shallots, sliced

1½ teaspoons kosher salt

1 teaspoon dried parsley

½ teaspoon dried basil

2 pounds snow peas

2 Tablespoons balsamic vinegar

1½ Tablespoons soy sauce

1. Heat oil in a large, deep frying pan over medium-high heat. Add shallots, salt, parsley, and basil. Sauté for 5-8 minutes, stirring occasionally, until softened.
2. Reduce heat to low; cook for at least 20 minutes, preferably 30-40, until the shallots are deeply caramelized.
3. Raise heat to high. Add snow peas, balsamic vinegar, and soy sauce. Stir fry, stirring often, for 3-4 minutes, until the snow peas are slightly softened but still crunchy.

Plan Ahead These snow peas are best enjoyed fresh. You can make them a day or two ahead and enjoy them later at room temperature. For best results, do not reheat.

Zucchini and Tomatoes
with Crispy Crumbs

Pareve | Yield 6-8 servings

This recipe may look simple, but don't let that fool you. The day we made these for the photoshoot, I intended to save them for Shabbos. But after a few people walked through my house during the shoot, I found two empty trays and lots of people begging for the recipe. They are just that good!

- **1 large** zucchini, cut into ¼-inch slices
- **4** plum tomatoes, cut into ¼-inch slices
- **¾ cup** panko crumbs
- **1 teaspoon** kosher salt
- **1 teaspoon** garlic powder
- **1 teaspoon** onion powder
- **1 teaspoon** paprika
- **4 teaspoons** olive oil

1. Preheat oven to 425°F. Line a baking sheet with parchment paper; coat well with nonstick cooking spray.
2. Line up vegetable slices in a single layer on prepared baking sheet; coat well with nonstick cooking spray.
3. In a small bowl, combine panko crumbs and spices. Stir to combine. Add oil; stir to form a slightly damp crumb mixture.
4. Divide the crumbs to cover each vegetable slice, pressing slightly to adhere.
5. Bake for about 40 minutes, until vegetables are cooked through and crispy on the outside.

Plan Ahead These veggies are best enjoyed fresh. You can make them a day or two ahead and enjoy them later at room temperature. For best results, do not reheat.

Garlic and Parsley Roasted Carrots

Pareve | Yield 4-6 servings

Sometimes I go through cooking phases, where despite my love for creating new recipes, I find myself making the same foods over and over and over again, for a long time. This is one of those dishes — there's a beauty in simplicity, and this recipe exemplifies that with the fresh garlic and parsley flavors.

4-6 large carrots cut into sticks; multicolored optional

1½ teaspoons kosher salt

¾ cup fresh parsley, finely chopped

12 cloves garlic, minced

¼ cup olive oil

4 teaspoons red wine vinegar

1. Preheat oven to 425°F. Line 2 baking sheets with parchment paper; set aside.

3. In a small bowl, combine salt, parsley, garlic, olive oil, and vinegar. Toss with carrot sticks until carrots are fully coated.

3. Place carrot sticks in a single layer on prepared baking sheets. Bake for about 40 minutes, flipping carrots halfway through, until lightly browned.

Plan Ahead This dish is best enjoyed fresh. You can make them a day or two ahead and enjoy them later at room temperature. For best results, do not reheat.

Variation Save time by using halved baby carrots; reduce baking time as needed.

Overnight Onions

Pareve | Yield 6 servings

This is my mother's specialty, and one of my favorite treats at her Shabbos table. Not only are these easy to make, but the long cook time makes them super sweet, super soft, and super delicious!

- **3 Tablespoons** olive oil
- **2 Tablespoons** balsamic vinegar
- **1 teaspoon** kosher salt
- **1 teaspoon** soy sauce
- **1 teaspoon** dried thyme
- **10-12** red onions, peeled and halved

1. Preheat oven to 275°F. Line a baking sheet with parchment paper; set aside.
2. Combine oil, vinegar, salt, soy sauce, and thyme in a small bowl. Whisk to combine.
3. Brush mixture generously over the cut sides of each onion half; place cut-side down on prepared baking sheet. Drizzle any remaining mixture over the onions.
4. Bake for 6-8 hours, up to overnight. Note that the outermost layer of the onion halves will become dried out and tough. Discard that layer before serving.

Plan Ahead The onions are best the day they are made. You can make them a day or two ahead and enjoy them later at room temperature. For best results, do not reheat.

Chili-Lime Brussels Sprouts

Pareve | Yield 6-8 servings

Looking for a new roasted veggie side dish your family will love? Try these Chili-Lime Brussels Sprouts — they're sweet, spicy, and so crispy!

2 (1-pound) bags frozen Brussels sprouts, defrosted

2 Tablespoons olive oil

2 Tablespoons pure maple syrup

zest and juice of **1** lime

1½ teaspoon chili powder

1½ teaspoons kosher salt

1. Preheat oven to 425°F. Line 2 baking sheets with parchment paper; set aside.
2. Use paper towels to squeeze as much excess water as possible from Brussels sprouts. Cut sprouts in half; place into a medium bowl.
3. Add remaining ingredients; toss to combine.
4. Place Brussels sprouts, cut side down, on prepared baking sheet, leaving room between each to help them crisp up. Bake for 35-40 minutes, until outsides are crispy.

Plan Ahead These are best enjoyed fresh. You can make them a day or two ahead and enjoy them later at room temperature. For best results, do not reheat.

Sweet Potato Wedges
with Avocado Drizzle

Pareve | Yield 6 servings

I always love a good sweet-and-savory recipe combo, and these sweet potatoes combined with the tangy avocado dip are no exception. As a bonus, the beautiful contrasting colors make it an eye-catching dish!

SWEET POTATO WEDGES

3 sweet potatoes

3 Tablespoons oil

1 teaspoon kosher salt

¼ teaspoon black pepper

AVOCADO DRIZZLE

1 avocado

½ cup mayonnaise

½ teaspoon kosher salt

1 teaspoon garlic powder

2 teaspoons lemon juice

1. Preheat oven to 425°F. Line 2 baking sheets with parchment paper; set aside.
2. Peel sweet potatoes and cut into wedges. Place into a large bowl; add oil, salt, and pepper. Toss to coat.
3. Place wedges in a single layer on prepared baking sheet. Bake for about 50 minutes, until the outsides are starting to brown.
4. **Meanwhile, prepare the avocado drizzle:** Place peeled and pitted avocado into a bowl; mash until smooth. Add remaining ingredients; stir to combine.
5. Remove roasted sweet potato from oven; allow to cool slightly. Just before serving, drizzle avocado mixture over wedges just before serving.

Plan Ahead Avocado drizzle can be prepared 2-3 days ahead. Due to the acid in the recipe, it should not turn brown. Sweet potato wedges are best fresh, but can be prepared a day or two ahead and served at room temperature.

Glazed Potatoes

Pareve | Yield 6-8 servings

This recipe is a Yom Tov staple in my home, and my family's favorite potato dish. My oven is never on over the holidays, so I created this stovetop potato dish as a way to enjoy a freshly made side dish at our special Yom Tov meals.

35-45 baby red potatoes, peel on

2 Tablespoons oil

GLAZE

½ cup duck sauce

¼ cup orange juice

¼ cup brown sugar

2 Tablespoons balsamic vinegar

1 Tablespoon soy sauce

1½ teaspoons kosher salt

½ teaspoon black pepper

1 teaspoon garlic powder

1 teaspoon sriracha (optional)

1. Boil potatoes in salted boiling water for about 15 minutes, until fork tender. Drain; set aside.
2. **Prepare the glaze:** Whisk together all ingredients in a medium bowl until smooth. Set aside.
3. Heat a large, deep frying pan over high heat. Add oil and potatoes. Cook, stirring often, until potatoes start to get crispy, about 5 minutes.
4. Reduce heat to medium. Pour glaze over potatoes and cook, stirring frequently, until glaze thickens and coats potatoes, about 8 minutes.

Plan Ahead Potatoes can be boiled 2-3 days ahead. Sauce can be prepared 2-3 days ahead. For best results, store each separately and follow Steps 3-4 on the day of use.

Corned Beef-Topped Smashed Potatoes

Meat | Yield 6-8 servings

Corned beef and potatoes are often served together, and in this fun twist, I've turned the classic combination into a beautiful and delicious side dish that you'll want to serve at your special occasion meals!

30 baby potatoes, peel on

1 Tablespoon oil

TOPPING

3 Tablespoons oil

3 onions, finely diced

1 teaspoon kosher salt

4 cloves garlic, minced

12 ounces sliced deli corned beef, diced

2 Tablespoons spicy brown mustard

1 Tablespoon soy sauce

1 Tablespoon brown sugar

2 teaspoons rice vinegar

1. **Prepare the potatoes:** Boil potatoes in salted boiling water for about 15 minutes, until fork tender. Drain; set aside.
2. Preheat oven to 400°F. Line a baking sheet with parchment paper; place boiled potatoes on baking sheet. Drizzle oil over potatoes; stir until all are coated. Place a second baking sheet over the potatoes and press down on it to smash each potato slightly. Set aside.
3. **Prepare the topping:** In a large, deep frying pan, heat oil over medium heat. Add onions and oil; sauté for about 5 minutes, until softened.
4. Add remaining ingredients; cook on medium-low heat, stirring occasionally, for 10-15 minutes, until onions are caramelized and flavors have deepened.
5. Place a large spoonful of corned beef mixture over each potato.
6. Bake for about 30 minutes, until potatoes are crispy.

Plan Ahead These potatoes are best fresh. If necessary, rewarm, loosely covered, until heated through.

Garlic Ginger Udon Noodles

Pareve | Yield 6-8 servings

This dish is a Yom Tov staple in my house, which is when I originally devised it. I like to prepare all of my holiday sides fresh, on Yom Tov, on the stove top. One year, I found delicious udon noodles in my grocery freezer (see Note), played around with flavors, and came up with this winner. Every Yom Tov, when these make an appearance at my table, my guests excitedly exclaim, "Yay! You made the udon noodles again!"

SAUCE

½ cup soy sauce

¼ cup rice vinegar

4 cloves garlic, minced

3 cubes frozen ginger

1 Tablespoon toasted sesame oil

¼ cup honey

ASSEMBLY

16-24 ounces udon noodles, cooked according to package directions

3-4 scallions, sliced, optional, for garnish

1 Tablespoon black and white sesame seeds, for garnish

1. Combine all sauce ingredients in a deep frying pan over high heat. Bring to a boil; reduce to a simmer. Cook until reduced and slightly thickened, at least 10 minutes.

2. Add cooked udon noodles to sauce, toss to fully coat. Cook and stir until heated through. Add scallions and sesame seeds just before serving, for garnish.

Note While any udon noodles will work for this dish, my personal favorite is the pre-cooked variety sold in the freezer aisle of many grocery stores. They are thick and chewy, and really complete this incredible dish.

Plan Ahead Sauce can be prepared up to a week ahead and stored in the fridge. Noodles can be prepared a couple of days ahead and stored in the fridge. Just before serving, reheat sauce, add noodles, and stir to warm through.

Lemon Quinoa with Pecans

Pareve | Yield 6 servings

The bright flavors and unique textures of this quinoa dish make a really fantastic and unique side dish.

- **2 Tablespoons** olive oil
- **1** onion, diced
- **2 teaspoon** kosher salt, divided
- **1** zucchini, diced
- **4 cloves** garlic, minced
- **1 teaspoon** fresh chopped basil OR **1 cube** frozen basil
- **1 Tablespoon** Dijon mustard
- **1 cup** raw quinoa
- **2¼ cups** water
- **⅓ cup** chopped toasted pecans
- juice of **1** lemon

1. Heat oil in a large, deep frying pan over medium heat. Add onion and half the salt. Cook for 5 minutes, until softened.
2. Add zucchini, garlic, basil, mustard, and remaining salt. Cook for 5-8 minutes, until softened.
3. Add quinoa and water; raise heat to high. Bring to a boil; lower heat. Simmer, covered, for about 15 minutes, until liquid is absorbed and quinoa is cooked through. Let rest for 5 minutes, then uncover and fluff with a fork. Stir in pecans and lemon juice.

Plan Ahead This dish can be prepared a day or two ahead. You can serve it at room temperature, or you can rewarm, covered, until heated through.

Baked Salami Rice

Meal | Yield 6-8 servings

I know that many people struggle with making perfectly cooked rice, and baking it seems to be the most foolproof solution. In this dish, I took the humble baked rice and turned it into an incredible dish that's worthy of your holiday and special occasion meals ... all while being easy enough for a weeknight dinner.

SALAMI

2 Tablespoons oil

1 onion, finely diced

2 cloves garlic, minced

1 teaspoon kosher salt

12 ounces salami, very finely diced

2 Tablespoons tomato paste

RICE

1½ cups basmati rice

3¼ cups water

1 teaspoon kosher salt

1. **Prepare the salami:** Heat oil in a large frying pan over medium heat. Add onion, garlic, and salt. Sauté for 8-10 minutes, until softened.
2. Stir in salami and tomato paste. Cook, stirring occasionally, for 10 minutes. Remove from heat.
3. Preheat oven to 350°F.
4. **Prepare the rice:** Place rice, water, and salt into a 9x13-inch baking dish. Add salami mixture; stir to combine. Cover tightly.
5. Bake for 1 hour. Remove from oven and let it rest, covered, for 10 minutes. Salami will rise to the top. Uncover; stir to incorporate salami just before serving.

Plan Ahead Prepare salami mixture and freeze. 1-2 days before serving, defrost salami mixture and proceed with recipe. Reheat, covered, until warmed through.

Potato Leek Knish Braid

Pareve | Yield 8 servings

If you're looking for a side dish that's got that "wow" factor, here you go! While this may seem complicated to make, don't be scared off! Not only is it freezer-friendly (!), but the dough is fantastically easy to make and work with!

FILLING

- 3 Tablespoons oil, divided
- 2 large onions, diced
- 1 Tablespoon kosher salt , divided
- ¼ teaspoon black pepper
- 3 large leeks, white and light green parts only, cut into half-moons
- 4 cloves garlic, minced
- 2 Tablespoons honey
- 5 Yukon Gold potatoes, boiled until fork-tender
- 1 egg, lightly beaten, for brushing

DOUGH

- 1½ cups flour
- 2 teaspoons sugar
- 1 teaspoon kosher salt
- 1 teaspoon baking powder
- 1 teaspoon vinegar
- ⅓ cup water

- 1 egg, lightly beaten

1. **Prepare the filling:** Heat half the oil in a large, deep frying pan over medium heat. Add onions, half the salt, and the pepper. Sauté for about 5 minutes, until softened.
2. Add leeks and garlic. Cook over medium heat for 5 minutes.
3. Reduce heat to low; add remaining oil, remaining salt, and honey. Cook for about 30 minutes, stirring every 10 minutes, until mixture has reduced and darkened slightly.
4. Use a potato masher or ricer to mash potatoes; place into a large bowl. Add onion mixture, stirring well to incorporate. Taste and adjust seasoning. Set aside.
5. Preheat oven to 375°F.
6. **Prepare the dough:** Combine all dough ingredients in a large bowl. Using an electric mixer, beat JUST until a smooth dough forms. Do not overmix.
7. **Prepare the braid:** On a large piece of parchment paper, roll dough out on a lightly floured surface into a rectangle, about 12 inches by 18 inches.
8. Lightly mark the dough into three sections along the length but do not cut it through. Place the filling along the center section.
9. Starting with one long side, cut parallel strips of dough, about 1-inch wide, from the edge of the filling toward the edge of the dough. Repeat with second side, cutting the same number of strips on each side.
10. To form the braid, angle a strip from one side over the filling, then repeat with a strip of dough from the other side. Repeat with remaining strips, alternating between the two sides, until the braid is complete.
11. Brush with beaten egg. Bake for 30-35 minutes, until golden bown.

Variation Change up the filling by omitting the leeks and placing strips of pastrami under the potato filling before braiding.

Plan Ahead This recipe can be prepared ahead and frozen, well wrapped, until ready to use. Rewarm, uncovered, until heated through.

Apple and Cabbage Noodle Kugel

Pareve | Yield 2 (9-inch) kugels, 6-8 portions each

Sweet and savory at its very best! Onions and cabbage provide a fabulous savory note, with apples, honey, and warm spices providing the perfect balance of sweetness. This is a great side dish to grace your next Shabbos or Rosh Hashanah meal.

- **2 Tablespoons** oil
- **1** onion, diced
- **2 teaspoons** kosher salt, divided
- **4 cloves** garlic, finely minced
- **16 ounces** shredded white cabbage
- **3** Granny Smith apples, peeled and cut into matchsticks
- **¼ teaspoon** ground ginger
- **2 teaspoons** cinnamon
- **2 Tablespoons** brown sugar
- juice of **1** lemon
- **8** eggs
- **⅓ cup** oil
- **⅓ cup** honey
- **1 teaspoon** vanilla extract
- **10 ounces** wide egg noodles, cooked according to package directions

1. Heat oil over medium-low heat in a large, deep frying pan. Add onions and 1 teaspoon salt; cook for about 10 minutes, until softened.
2. Add garlic, cabbage, and remaining teaspoon salt. Cook for 8 minutes, until softened.
3. Reduce heat to low. Add apples, ginger, cinnamon, brown sugar, and lemon juice. Cook over low heat, stirring occasionally, for at least 20 minutes, preferably 30-40 minutes for best flavor, until mixture has deep brown color. Transfer to a bowl; set aside to cool.
4. Preheat oven to 350°F. Grease 2 (9-inch) round pans; set aside.
5. Combine cooled apple and cabbage mixture with eggs, oil, honey, and vanilla.
6. Add noodles; stir to combine.
7. Divide mixture between prepared pans. Bake about 50 minutes, until golden brown and the tops feel firm.

Plan Ahead Kugels can be prepared ahead and frozen until ready to serve. Reheat, loosely covered, until warmed through.

Two-Ingredient Sides

Pareve | Yield each about 6 servings

As a cookbook author who likes to share easy, approachable recipes, I sometimes struggle with the idea of how easy is TOO easy to consider it a recipe? My solution: Here's a roundup of my favorite barely-a-recipe, only-two-ingredient (not counting oil and salt!) side dishes that will blow your mind, despite the short ingredient list!

1. Preheat oven to 425°F. Line a baking sheet with parchment paper.
2. Combine all ingredients for your desired dish on baking sheet. Toss to combine.
3. Spread in a single layer; bake for the time listed, stirring or flipping halfway through.

EVERYTHING EGGPLANT

30-40 minutes

2 large eggplants, sliced

2 teaspoons kosher salt

1 Tablespoon olive oil

2 Tablespoons everything bagel spice mix (page 290) or store-bought

GARLICKY BROCCOLI

25-30 minutes for fresh/ 30-55 minutes for frozen

12 ounces broccoli florets, cut into bite-size pieces

8-10 cloves garlic, very thinly sliced

1 teaspoon kosher salt

3 Tablespoons olive oil

SHAWARMA SPICED POTATOES

30-35 minutes

4-6 Idaho potatoes, peeled and cubed

2 teaspoons kosher salt

3 Tablespoons olive oil

2 Tablespoons shawarma spice

PESTO ROASTED ZUCCHINI

40 minutes

2 large zucchini, sliced

¼ cup pesto (page 292) or store-bought

2 Tablespoons olive oil

½ teaspoon kosher salt

ZAATAR CABBAGE

30 minutes

14-16 ounces shredded white cabbage

1 teaspoon kosher salt

2 Tablespoons zaatar

2 Tablespoons olive oil

STRAWBERRY SHORTCAKE CHEESECAKE TRIFLES, PAGE 232

S'MORES MARTINI, PAGE 252
TROPICAL BLUE PUNCH, PAGE 253

CARAMEL APPLE COOKIE PIE, PAGE 240

CITRUS PLATTER WITH PISTACHIO AND MINT DRESSING, PAGE 250

PEANUT BUTTER TIRAMISU, PAGE 234

NO-BAKE S'MORES CHEESECAKE, PAGE 242

Desserts *and* Drinks

Two-Ingredient Chocolate Mousse

Dairy or Pareve | Yield 8 servings

When my good friend had a baby boy on Friday morning (it often seems that baby boys are all born on Friday morning!), I wanted to make something really quick and easy for their Shalom Zachor that night. I went through my cabinets and found these two ingredients, and, well, life has never been the same. This two-ingredient chocolate mousse is incredible just plain, but it's also infinitely customizable, with four fantastic options listed below.

1 (16-ounce) container nondairy whip

1 (13-14 ounce) jar dairy or pareve chocolate hazelnut spread

1. In the bowl of an electric mixer fitted with the whisk attachment, beat whip on high speed until stiff peaks form.
2. Turn mixer speed to low; add chocolate spread. Beat until just combined. Serve chilled.

MOUSSE-TOPPED BROWNIE

Pipe or spoon chocolate mousse over a piece of Brownie Cake (page 276) or your favorite brownie or cake. Top with chocolate garnishes, if desired.

TRADITIONAL

Serve mousse in a glass or Mason jar, topped with whipped cream or pareve whipped cream, chocolate shavings, and fresh fruit, if desired.

ICE CREAM PIE

Divide mousse between 2 store-bought graham cracker pie crusts. Top with Cereal Crunch Chocolate Crumbs (page 294) or chocolate sprinkles. Freeze until solid, then cut into slices to serve.

MOUSSE TRIFLE

In a tall, narrow glass, pipe alternating layers of chocolate mousse with another flavor of mousse, such as Cheesecake Mousse (page 232) or Cookies and Cream (page 238).

Strawberry Shortcake Cheesecake Trifles

Dairy or Pareve | Yield 12-15 trifles

This is one of my staple desserts, both when cooking for my family and friends, and when traveling around giving cooking demos. What's not to love? Not only is this an impressive looking dessert, but it's easy to make and bursting with flavor!

POUND CAKE

1 stick (½ cup) butter OR oil

2 eggs

1 cup sugar

1 teaspoon vanilla extract

1 cup flour

½ cup milk OR nondairy milk

STRAWBERRY SAUCE

1 pound frozen strawberries

2 Tablespoons lemon juice

⅓ cup sugar

CHEESECAKE MOUSSE:

1 cup heavy whipping cream OR nondairy whipped topping

1 (8-ounce) bar brick cream cheese OR nondairy cream cheese

1 teaspoon vanilla extract

⅓ cup powdered sugar

1. **Prepare the pound cake:** Preheat oven to 350°F. Line a rimmed baking sheet with parchment paper (see Note); set aside.
2. In the bowl of an electric mixer, combine butter, eggs, sugar, and vanilla, beating until smooth. Beating to combine after each addition, add half the flour, half the milk, remaining flour, then remaining milk. Spread batter onto prepared baking sheet (don't spread all the way to the rim or it will be too thin — the batter should cover about ¾ of the pan).
3. Bake for 15 minutes. Allow to cool completely before assembling trifles.
4. **Prepare the strawberry sauce:** Combine all filling ingredients in a pot; bring to a boil. Reduce heat; simmer, stirring occasionally, for 15-20 minutes, or until thickened. If the strawberries are still whole, break them up with a spoon. Let cool completely before assembling trifles. If a smoother sauce is desired, purée strawberry mixture.
5. **Prepare the cheesecake mousse:** In the bowl of an electric mixer fitted with the whisk attachment, beat cream until stiff. Add cream cheese, vanilla, and powdered sugar. (If mixture is not thick enough to pipe, refrigerate for 1-2 hours before piping.)
6. Place a slice of cake into each dessert dish. Top with strawberry sauce; pipe on a layer of cheesecake mousse. Serve cold.

Note Baking the cake on the rimmed baking sheet produces a very thin cake that is best for layering, but it can also be baked in a 9x13-inch pan. Bake for 25 minutes, then proceed with the recipe.

Plan Ahead Assembled trifles can be frozen in air tight containers.

Peanut Butter Tiramisu

Dairy or Pareve | Yield 8-10 servings

*I've been hooked on the combination of peanut butter and coffee ever since I worked on the Peanut Butter Iced Mocha Recipe for **Real Life Kosher Cooking**. In this beautiful dessert, I used that wonderful flavor combination to give a traditional dessert a new twist!*

PEANUT BUTTER CREAM

2 cups heavy whipping cream OR nondairy whipped topping

¾ cup creamy peanut butter

1 (8-ounce) bar brick cream cheese OR nondairy cream cheese

1 (3.5-ounce) package instant vanilla pudding mix

¾ cup brown sugar

1 teaspoon vanilla extract

2 Tablespoons prepared coffee

SOAKING LIQUID

1 cup prepared strong coffee

¼ cup amaretto liqueur

2 Tablespoons brown sugar

ASSEMBLY

1½ (7-ounce) packages ladyfinger cookies

1 (3½-ounce) dark chocolate bar, shaved into curls, for garnish

1. **Prepare peanut butter cream:** In the bowl of an electric mixer fitted with the whisk attachment, beat cream until stiff peaks form. Remove to a separate bowl. There's no need to wash the mixer bowl before continuing.
2. Place peanut butter, cream cheese, instant pudding mix, sugar, vanilla, and coffee into mixer bowl. Beat until combined and creamy.
3. With the mixer on low, gently add back half of the reserved cream. Beat until just incorporated; then repeat with remaining cream. Set aside.
4. **Prepare soaking liquid:** Whisk together all soaking liquid ingredients in a small bowl until combined.
5. **Assemble tiramisu:** Working with one at a time, dip a cookie into the soaking liquid until fully submerged, then place into a dessert dish, glass, or jar. Repeat to form a layer of cookies. Spoon or pipe a layer of peanut butter cream over cookies, then continue to dip and place another layer of dipped cookies and another layer of cream. Repeat with remaining dishes, layering dipped cookies with cream.
6. Top each serving with chocolate curls.

Variation Instead of individual desserts, as pictured, you can layer the cookies and cream in a large trifle bowl.

Plan Ahead Peanut butter cream can be prepared ahead and frozen. Tiramisu can be prepared 1-2 days ahead of time.

Orange Bourbon Ice Cream Trifle

Dairy or Pareve | Yield 8-10 servings

"I don't know what this is," my friend's husband said after I served this for dessert after Shabbos lunch. "But it tastes very American. And really good." He proceeded to have a second and third serving, as did everyone else at the table. The alcohol in the bourbon keeps the ice cream from freezing solid, which makes for a creamy, almost soft-serve texture.

ORANGE BOURBON MIXTURE

zest of **1 large** orange

juice of **1 large** orange

½ cup apple cider

⅓ cup bourbon

1 teaspoon cinnamon

pinch ground cloves

pinch kosher salt

ICE CREAM

1 (56-ounce) container dairy OR pareve vanilla ice cream

½ cup powdered sugar

½ teaspoon vanilla extract

GARNISH

2½ cups graham cracker crumbs

1-2 oranges, sliced, optional, for garnish

1. **Prepare the orange bourbon mixture:** In a medium bowl, whisk together orange zest, juice, apple cider, bourbon, cinnamon, cloves, and salt until combined.
2. **Prepare the ice cream:** Place ice cream into the bowl of a food processor fitted with the "S" blade; add powdered sugar and vanilla.
3. Reserve ¼-cup orange bourbon mixture for the graham cracker crumbs; add remaining mixture to the food processor. Process mixture until it's completely smooth, and no hints of white (unmixed ice cream) are visible.
4. **Prepare the garnish:** Combine graham cracker crumbs with reserved bourbon mixture, forming crumbs with the texture of damp sand.
5. **To assemble:** Layer graham cracker crumb mixture and ice cream in trifle glasses. Freeze until ready to serve. If desired, place an orange slice on the rim of each glass just before serving (not shown).

Variation For an ultra-easy version of this dessert, divide the ice cream mixture between 2 graham cracker crusts. Top with graham cracker crumb mixture.

Plan Ahead Freeze trifles, well covered, until ready to serve.

Cookies and Cream Krembos

Pareve | Yield 20 krembos

Krembos, a favorite Israeli treat, have a cookie base, a mound of cream on top, and a chocolate coating over it all. I made this playful take on that favorite treat with cookies and cream flavors throughout, both in the base and in the mousse topping. Feel free to serve it the traditional way — in a cup. I like to garnish it with a mini chocolate sandwich cookie!

COOKIES AND CREAM MOUSSE

1 cup nondairy whip, not whipped

1 teaspoon vanilla extract

⅔ cup Marshmallow Fluff

1 cup finely chopped chocolate sandwich cookies (about 8 whole cookies)

BASE

20 chocolate sandwich cookies

TOPPING

12 ounces semi-sweet chocolate, chopped

1-2 teaspoons oil, as needed

1. **Prepare the cookies and cream mousse:** In the bowl of an electric mixer fitted with the whisk attachment, beat whip on high speed until stiff peaks form.
2. Add vanilla and Marshmallow Fluff; beat until combined and smooth. Remove bowl from mixer; stir in chopped cookies.
3. Place the mousse into a piping bag without a tip (cookies will get stuck in a tip). Pipe a high swirl of mousse over each chocolate sandwich cookie. Place in freezer for 1-2 hours, until firm.
4. **Prepare the topping:** In a small heatproof bowl fitted over a pot of boiling water, melt chocolate and oil together until melted and smooth.
5. Dip frozen mousse swirls into melted chocolate, covering it completely. Place in fridge or freezer to harden. Krembo can be served straight from the freezer, or at room temperature.

Variation Instead of forming krembos, as described here, pipe or spoon the mousse into glasses and serve as mousse cups. I like to top them with mini sandwich cookies and/or a sprinkle of cookie crumbs for garnish.

Plan Ahead These treats can be prepared ahead and frozen until ready to use.

Caramel Apple Cookie Pie

Pareve | Yield 8 servings

This dessert is light and refreshing, and a great way to update a classic. It's delicious cold on a hot summer day and equally delicious served warm on a chilly evening. And that crunch? Unlike anything you've had before!

- **⅔ cup** oil
- **½ cup** brown sugar
- **2** eggs
- **1 (3.5-ounce) package** vanilla instant pudding mix
- **1 teaspoon** baking powder
- **1 teaspoon** vanilla extract
- **pinch** kosher salt
- **1⅓ cups** flour
- **1** apple, peeled and finely diced
- **½ cup** caramel or butterscotch chips
- **1** graham cracker pie crust

OPTIONAL TOPPINGS

- caramel sauce, store-bought, optional
- pareve ice cream, optional

1. Preheat oven to 350°F.
2. In the bowl of an electric mixer on medium speed, beat together oil, sugar, eggs, pudding mix, baking powder, vanilla, and salt. Beat until combined and creamy.
3. Turn mixer speed to low. Add flour; beat until just combined. Stir in apples and caramel chips.
4. Carefully pour mixture into pie crust. Bake for 45-50 minutes, until the center is set.
5. Drizzle with caramel sauce. Serve with a scoop of ice cream, if desired.

Plan Ahead This pie can be frozen, well wrapped.

No-Bake S'mores Cheesecake

Dairy | Yield 1 (9-inch) cheescake; 10-12 servings

Often, no-bake cheesecakes are served soft-serve style, in a glass or a mini cup. But not this one! This cheesecake gets its firmness from the melted marshmallows — which, naturally, made me think of S'mores. A graham cracker crust and rich chocolate topping complete the flavor trifecta. And by the way, this is perfect for those of us who don't have a dairy oven.

CRUST

1½ cups graham cracker crumbs

¼ cup sugar

6 Tablespoons butter, melted

BATTER

2½ cups heavy whipping cream, divided

3 (8-ounce) bars brick cream cheese

1½ teaspoons vanilla extract

2 (8-ounce) bags large marshmallows

FUDGE TOPPING

½ cup heavy whipping cream

1 (3.5-ounce) bar milk chocolate

8 ounces dark chocolate

toasted marshmallows, optional, for garnish (see Note)

1. **Prepare the crust:** In a medium bowl, mix together the graham cracker crumbs, sugar, and melted butter until combined. (It will have the texture of wet sand.) Press along the bottom and up the sides of a 9-inch springform pan. Press a round measuring cup along the edge to smooth it out. Place the crust in the freezer while you prepare the batter.
2. **Prepare the batter:** In a large bowl, use an electric mixer to beat ½ cup cream until stiff. Add cream cheese; beat for a few minutes until the mixture is smooth and creamy. Add vanilla; beat until incorporated. Set aside.
3. In a medium pot over medium heat, melt together the marshmallows and remaining cream until melted and smooth. Stir frequently. This should take 2-3 minutes. Set aside to cool for about 5 minutes; stir into the cream cheese mixture.
4. Pour the batter into the prepared crust. Refrigerate for a few hours until set.
5. **Prepare the fudge topping:** Combine all topping ingredients in a heatproof bowl fitted over a small pot of boiling water. Melt over medium heat, stirring occasionally, until melted and smooth. Set aside to cool for a few minutes, then pour over cooled cheesecake. Place in fridge till firm. Top with toasted marshmallows, if using.

Note While not necessary, the toasted marshmallow garnish pictured adds great flavor and a fun aspect — not to mention authenticity — to this dessert. To make them, simply thread marshmallows on a skewer and roast over a flame (I used a stove burner) until they catch fire. Blow out the flame; set aside to cool.

Chocolate Cherry Tart

Dairy or Pareve | Yield 8-10 servings

Chocolate and cherry are a classic pairing, for good reason. The rich and flaky chocolate crust of this dessert is complimented by the fruitiness of the cherry filling — which has a chocolate surprise, too!

DOUGH

1½ cups flour

2 Tablespoons cocoa powder

⅓ cup powdered sugar

pinch sea salt

1 egg yolk

1 cup (2 sticks) frozen butter OR margarine, cubed

3-6 Tablespoons ice water

CHOCOLATE CHERRY FILLING

4 cups cherries, fresh or frozen, pitted

⅓ cup sugar

juice of 1 lemon

2 Tablespoons cocoa powder

2 Tablespoons cornstarch

⅓ cup water

fresh cherries optional, for garnish

chocolate shavings, optional, for garnish

1. **Prepare the dough:** Place flour, cocoa, sugar, and salt into the bowl of a food processor fitted with the "S" blade. Pulse a few times to combine.
2. Add egg yolk and cubed butter. Pulse in quick on/off bursts a few times, until the mixture forms coarse, uneven crumbs.
3. Sprinkle 3 tablespoons ice water over the top; pulse another few times, JUST until the mixture comes together. Add more water if necessary. Do not overmix. It will still be crumbly at this point; the dough will come together as it chills.
4. Wrap the dough in plastic wrap; refrigerate for 2-3 hours, up to overnight.
5. **Prepare the chocolate cherry filling:** Combine all filling ingredients in a medium pot. Stir to combine. Bring mixture to a boil over high heat; reduce heat and simmer for 10-15 minutes, until thickened. Remove from heat; set aside to cool.
6. **Assemble the tart:** Preheat oven to 350°F. Roll chilled dough out on a lightly floured surface to about ¼-inch thickness. Press into a 9-inch tart pan. Trim and reserve the excess dough.
7. Pour filling into tart pan. Use extra dough to create lines, lattice, or decorations along the top.
8. Bake for 35-40 minutes, until the crust feels firm and the cherry juice is bubbling through.
9. Garnish with fresh cherries and chocolate shavings, if desired.

Plan Ahead This tart freezes nicely, well wrapped. For best results, reheat (uncovered) before serving.

Fudge-Filled Chocolate Wontons

Dairy or Pareve | Yield 40-50 wontons

If you've always thought of wontons only as a savory treat, think again! Wonton wrappers are neutral in flavor and therefore work with pretty much any filling. I've made all kinds of dessert wontons in the past — using cookie dough filling, apple pie filling, etc. — but these fudgy chocolate wontons are a definite favorite for all chocoholics!

15 ounces semi-sweet chocolate, chopped

1 (8-ounce) bar brick cream cheese OR nondairy cream cheese

2 eggs, lightly beaten

⅔ cup sugar

1 teaspoon vanilla extract

40-50 wonton wrappers

oil, for frying OR nonstick cooking spray

strawberry sauce OR jam, optional, for serving

powdered sugar, optional, for serving

whipped cream, optional, for serving

1. Place a heatproof bowl over a pot of boiling water. Reduce heat to medium-low; add chocolate. Heat until chocolate is fully melted.
2. Add cream cheese, eggs, and sugar. Stir quickly, so eggs don't scramble, until mixture is fully melted, combined, and smooth. Remove from heat; stir in vanilla extract. Set mixture aside for about 5 minutes, until slightly cooled and thickened.
3. Place about a teaspoon of filling in the center of a wonton wrapper, then dip a finger into a cup of water, wet edges of wonton wrapper. Fold it up and press to seal. Repeat with remaining wontons and filling.
4. **Deep Fried Method:** Heat about 1 inch of oil in a large, deep frying pan. Add wontons; cook for 2-3 minutes, until golden and crispy. Drain on paper towels.

   Air Fryer Method: Spray both sides of each wonton well; place in air fryer basket. Cook at 430°F for 8 minutes.

   Oven Method: Preheat oven to 425°F. Line a baking sheet with parchment paper. Coat each wonton really well with nonstick baking spray; place on prepared baking sheet. Bake for 8-10 minutes, until crispy.
5. Serve hot, with a sprinkle of powdered sugar and a drizzle of strawberry sauce (page 232), and whipped cream, if desired.

Plan Ahead Wontons can be baked and frozen until ready for use. Reheat, uncovered, before serving.

Sesame Apple Crumble
with Halva Crumbs

Pareve | Yield 10 servings

The familiar flavors of the humble apple crumble are really kicked up a notch with the surprising addition of sesame — in two forms. This is just the kind of recipe I love to share: familiar, but with a new and exciting twist!

HALVA CRUMBS

- 2½ cups flour
- ¾ cup sugar
- ¾ cup shredded halva
- 1 teaspoon baking powder
- ¼ teaspoon sea salt
- 1 egg
- 6 Tablespoons oil

APPLE MIXTURE

- 5 Granny Smith apples, peeled and sliced
- 2 Tablespoons tahini paste
- 2 Tablespoons silan OR honey
- juice of 1 lemon
- ½ cup sugar

1. Preheat oven to 350°F. Coat 10 ramekins with nonstick cooking spray; set aside.
2. **Prepare the halva crumbs:** In a medium bowl, combine flour, sugar, halva, baking powder, and salt. Add egg and oil; stir to form coarse, damp crumbs that stick together when squeezed. Set aside.
3. **Prepare apple mixture:** In a large bowl, combine apples, tahini, silan, lemon juice, and sugar. Toss to coat evenly.
4. Place a small amount of crumbs into each ramekin. Divide the apple mixture among the ramekins, then top each with remaining crumbs, filling to the top of the ramekins.
5. Bake for about 25 minutes, until crumbs feel firm. Serve warm for best results.

Variation To make one large crumble, place about ¼ of the crumbs into a 9x13-inch pan coated with nonstick cooking spray. Add apple mixture; top evenly with remaining crumbs. Bake for about 45 minutes.

Plan Ahead Crumble can be frozen, well wrapped, until ready for use. Reheat, uncovered, until heated through.

Citrus Platter
with Pistachios and Mint Dressing

Pareve | Yield 4-6 servings

After a Yom Tov meal filled with so many delicacies, I often like to serve a simple dessert, such as a fruit platter, to end the meal off on a lighter note. This simple citrus platter fits that bill perfectly: It's light and beautiful and so refreshing.

4 oranges, preferably of different varieties/colors (see Note)

2 grapefruits, preferably of different varieties/colors

½ cup roasted salted pistachios, chopped

DRESSING

⅓ cup honey

juice of **2** limes

juice of **1** lemon

2 teaspoons finely chopped mint

1. Peel and slice oranges and grapefruits; arrange on a platter. Set aside.
2. **Prepare the dressing:** Whisk together all dressing ingredients in a small bowl.
3. Drizzle dressing over sliced fruit.
4. Sprinkle chopped pistachios over the fruit just before serving.

Note For maximum flavor and prettiest presentation, try to use assorted varieties of both fruits, such as white and ruby red grapefruit, and a variety of oranges, such as blood oranges and Cara Cara, in addition to navel oranges.

Variation Make a seasonal adaptation of this recipe by using slices of any fruit that's in season in place of the citrus.

Plan Ahead Dressing can be prepared a few days ahead. Platter should be assembled fresh.

S'mores Martini

Dairy or Pareve | Yield 2 servings

What happens when you combine nostalgic childhood memories of a bonfire with a delicious adult beverage? This. And it's just as tasty as you'd expect, and then some!

2 ounces caramel vodka

1 ounce vanilla vodka

2 ounces chocolate liqueur

2 ounces heavy whipping cream OR nondairy whipped topping

ice cubes

graham cracker crumbs, marshmallows and chocolate syrup, optional, for garnish

mini skewers or long toothpicks

1. Combine all ingredients in a cocktail shaker with ice. Shake until well mixed and chilled.
2. **To garnish:** Dip the rim of martini glasses into chocolate syrup, then into graham cracker crumbs. Strain cocktail into glasses.
3. Thread a marshmallow onto a skewer or toothpick. Use flame of a stove or kitchen torch to scorch them. Drape skewer over top of glass just before serving. Repeat for second serving.

Note If you don't have both caramel and vanilla vodka, use the full amount of just one, or use plain vodka and add a dash of vanilla extract.

Blue Punch

Pareve | Yield 2 servings

This is my signature cocktail, and by far my most requested. Close your eyes and let it take you away to a stress-free tropical island!

1 ounce triple sec

2 ounces rum

2 ounces blue curaçao

2-3 ounces passion fruit juice, to taste

2 ounces pineapple juice

2 teaspoons lime juice

ice cubes OR crushed ice

fruit for garnish, optional

1. Combine all ingredients in a cocktail shaker; shake well with ice.
2. Strain into glasses. Garnish with fruit of your choice, if desired.

Note Blue curaçao is liqueur made from a bitter orange grown on the island of Curaçao. Its signature color adds a whimsical touch to this, as well as to other cocktail recipes. It's available with a hechsher from a number of brands, including Leroux.

Maple Walnut Frappe

Dairy or Pareve | Yield 2-3 servings

Sweet, nutty, rich, and creamy, this frappe is better than anything you'll get at your local coffee shop!

- **⅓ cup** boiling water
- **2 Tablespoons** instant coffee granules
- **¼ cup** toasted walnuts (see Note)
- **¼ cup** pure maple syrup
- **¼ teaspoon** vanilla extract
- **1½ cup** milk OR nondairy milk
- **2½ cups** (heaping) ice cubes
- sugar OR sweetener, optional, to taste

- chopped nuts, optional, for garnish
- whipped cream, optional, for garnish

1. Combine water and instant coffee in a blender. Cool for 5 minutes.
2. Add remaining ingredients; blend until smooth. If desired, add sugar to taste.

Note You can buy toasted walnuts or, to toast walnuts yourself, spread nuts on a parchment-lined baking sheet. Bake at 350°F for 10-12 minutes, stirring halfway through. Allow to cool before adding to frappe.

Plan Ahead This drink is best enjoyed fresh.

Strawberry Chocolate Milkshake

Dairy | Yield 2-3 servings

Chocolate and strawberries are a classic combination of flavors — for a great reason. This rich and creamy milkshake is the perfect way to highlight them both!

2 cups (1 pint) chocolate ice cream

¼ cup strawberry jam

2 heaping cups frozen strawberries

1 Tablespoon cocoa powder

1¼-1½ cups milk

whipped cream, optional, for garnish

chocolate and/or strawberry syrup, optional, for garnish

1. Place ice cream, jam, strawberries, cocoa powder, and 1¼ cups milk into a blender. Process until smooth.
2. If necessary, add up to an additional ¼ cup milk to reach desired consistency.
3. Garnish with whipped cream and chocolate and/or strawberry syrup, if desired.

Plan Ahead Milkshakes are best enjoyed fresh.

GLAZED LIME COOKIES, PAGE 262

BUTTERSCOTCH SWIRL BUNDT CAKE, PAGE 274

CANDIED PECAN BISCOTTI, PAGE 268

CARAMEL MACCHIATO RUGELACH, PAGE 282

CHERRY CHEESECAKE CUMB CAKE, PAGE 278

STONE FRUIT STICKY BUNS, PAGE 280

Baked Goods *and* Pastries

Peanut Butter Crinkle Cookies

Pareve | Yield about 3 dozen cookies

This recipe is for my sister-in-law Freidi, who once complained to me that many peanut butter cookie recipes were disappointingly light on peanut butter flavor. Well, let me assure you, these gorgeous peanut butter crinkles are the exact opposite. They're rich and simply bursting with peanut butter flavor in every bite — a real peanut butter lover's dream!

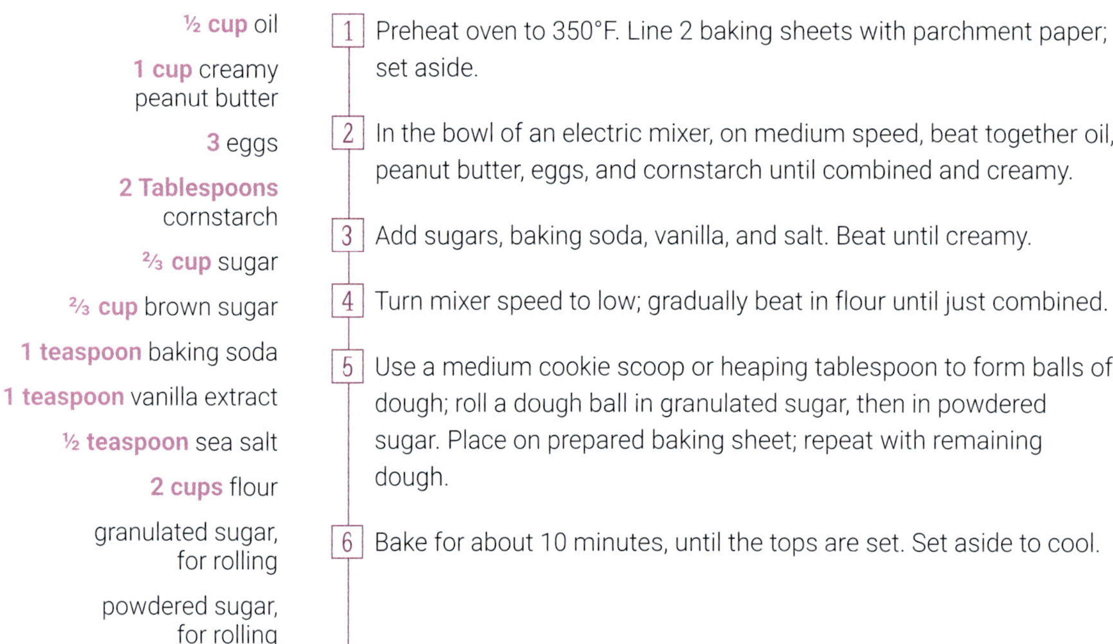

½ cup oil

1 cup creamy peanut butter

3 eggs

2 Tablespoons cornstarch

⅔ cup sugar

⅔ cup brown sugar

1 teaspoon baking soda

1 teaspoon vanilla extract

½ teaspoon sea salt

2 cups flour

granulated sugar, for rolling

powdered sugar, for rolling

1. Preheat oven to 350°F. Line 2 baking sheets with parchment paper; set aside.
2. In the bowl of an electric mixer, on medium speed, beat together oil, peanut butter, eggs, and cornstarch until combined and creamy.
3. Add sugars, baking soda, vanilla, and salt. Beat until creamy.
4. Turn mixer speed to low; gradually beat in flour until just combined.
5. Use a medium cookie scoop or heaping tablespoon to form balls of dough; roll a dough ball in granulated sugar, then in powdered sugar. Place on prepared baking sheet; repeat with remaining dough.
6. Bake for about 10 minutes, until the tops are set. Set aside to cool.

Plan Ahead Cookies can be frozen until ready to serve. Powdered sugar coating may dissolve, but the flavor will not be affected.

MILK

Glazed Lime Cookies

Pareve | Yield about 2 dozen cookies

I love watching people taste these for the first time, because they don't even know what to exclaim over first: the incredibly delicate texture or the fresh lime bursting through with every bite. It may seem like extra work to squeeze fresh lime juice, but believe me when I tell you ... it's worth every minute when you taste the final product.

1 cup oil

1½ cups sugar

¼ cup freshly squeezed lime juice

1 teaspoon baking powder

1 teaspoon vanilla extract

zest of **2** limes, 1 teaspoon reserved for the glaze

1 egg

3 cups flour

GLAZE

1 cup powdered sugar

1 teaspoon reserved lime zest

4 teaspoons freshly squeezed lime juice

1. Preheat oven to 350°F. Line cookie sheets with parchment paper; set aside.
2. In the bowl of an electric mixer on medium speed, beat oil and sugar until combined.
3. Add lime juice, baking powder, vanilla, lime zest, and egg. Beat until creamy.
4. Turn mixer speed to low. Add flour; beat until combined.
5. Using a small cookie scoop, scoop the dough onto prepared cookie sheets.
6. Bake for 9 minutes. Set aside to cool completely before glazing.
7. **Prepare the glaze:** Stir together all glaze ingredients in a bowl until combined.
8. Drizzle glaze over cooled cookies.

Plan Ahead These cookies freeze nicely, well wrapped.

Cookie Crunch Confetti Cookies

Pareve | Yield 2 dozen cookies

As a good aunt, I have a box full of sprinkles, colored sugar, and other toppings. I am always ready to lead a fun activity when the kids come over. The kids helped me come up with this fun and colorful cookie concept – and then they helped me make it.

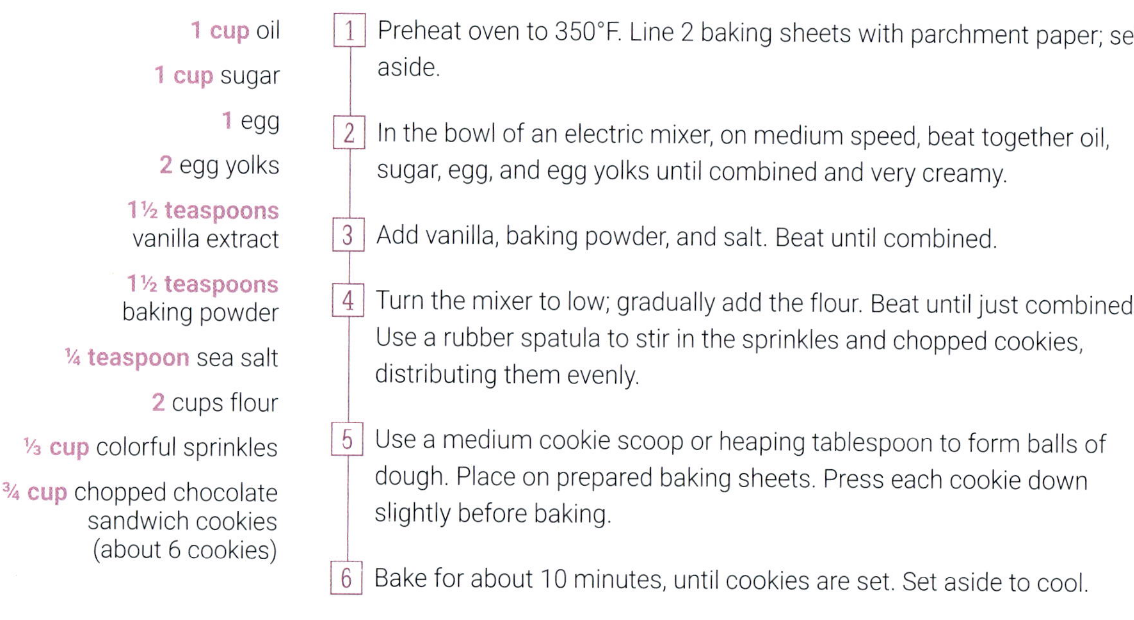

1 cup oil
1 cup sugar
1 egg
2 egg yolks
1½ teaspoons vanilla extract
1½ teaspoons baking powder
¼ teaspoon sea salt
2 cups flour
⅓ cup colorful sprinkles
¾ cup chopped chocolate sandwich cookies (about 6 cookies)

1. Preheat oven to 350°F. Line 2 baking sheets with parchment paper; set aside.
2. In the bowl of an electric mixer, on medium speed, beat together oil, sugar, egg, and egg yolks until combined and very creamy.
3. Add vanilla, baking powder, and salt. Beat until combined.
4. Turn the mixer to low; gradually add the flour. Beat until just combined. Use a rubber spatula to stir in the sprinkles and chopped cookies, distributing them evenly.
5. Use a medium cookie scoop or heaping tablespoon to form balls of dough. Place on prepared baking sheets. Press each cookie down slightly before baking.
6. Bake for about 10 minutes, until cookies are set. Set aside to cool.

Plan Ahead These cookies freeze nicely, well wrapped.

Jumbo Chocolate Sea Salt Cookies

Pareve | Yield 6-8 jumbo cookies

Sometimes you just need an indulgent treat ... that's when it's time to supersize your chocolate cookie!

1 cup oil
1 cup sugar
½ cup brown sugar
2 eggs
1 teaspoon baking soda
1 teaspoon sea salt
1 teaspoon vanilla extract
6 ounces semi-sweet OR bittersweet chocolate, melted and cooled for a few minutes
¾ cup cocoa powder
1½ cups flour
large-grain salt, preferably sea salt flakes, such as Waldon

1. Preheat oven to 350°F. Line 3 baking sheets with parchment paper; set aside.
2. In the bowl of an electric mixer on medium speed, beat together oil, sugars, and eggs for 2-3 minutes, until creamy.
3. Stir in baking soda, salt, vanilla, and melted chocolate.
4. Turn mixer speed to low; add cocoa and flour. Beat until just combined.
5. Use a ½-cup measuring cup to scoop out dough. Form into a ball; then flatten slightly and place on prepared baking sheet. Repeat with remaining dough. Don't bake more than 3 cookies per sheet, to allow room for spreading. Sprinkle cookies with sea salt.
6. Bake for 18-20 minutes, until cookies are set. Allow to cool before removing them from the baking sheet.

Variation Use a medium scoop or a heaping tablespoon to make regular-size cookies. Bake 8-10 minutes.

Plan Ahead These cookies freeze well in an airtight container or bag.

Candied Pecan Biscotti

Pareve | Yield 2-2½ dozen cookies

*As with so many of my great desserts, such as the Hot Gooey Caramel Pie in **Something Sweet**, this recipe was created for a family member who doesn't like chocolate. I was looking for a cookie mix-in that wasn't chocolate and that wasn't the usual (caramel chips and the like). I hit on the idea of using candied nuts, and everyone agreed that it was a phenomenal change — chocolate lover or not!*

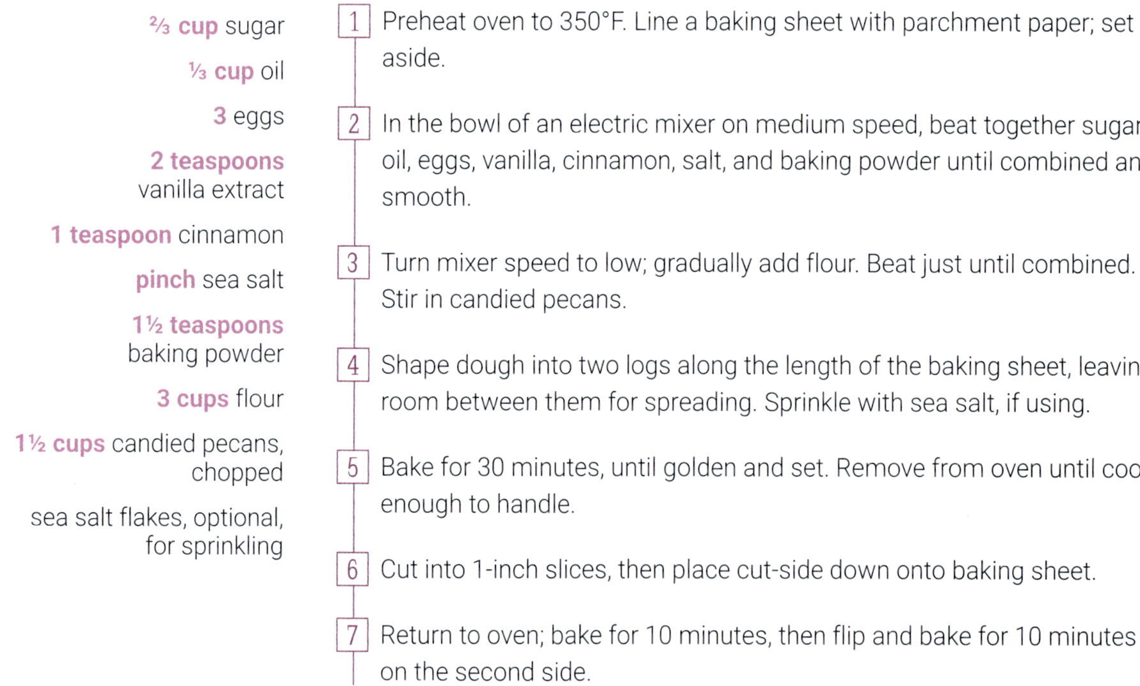

- **⅔ cup** sugar
- **⅓ cup** oil
- **3** eggs
- **2 teaspoons** vanilla extract
- **1 teaspoon** cinnamon
- **pinch** sea salt
- **1½ teaspoons** baking powder
- **3 cups** flour
- **1½ cups** candied pecans, chopped
- sea salt flakes, optional, for sprinkling

1. Preheat oven to 350°F. Line a baking sheet with parchment paper; set aside.
2. In the bowl of an electric mixer on medium speed, beat together sugar, oil, eggs, vanilla, cinnamon, salt, and baking powder until combined and smooth.
3. Turn mixer speed to low; gradually add flour. Beat just until combined. Stir in candied pecans.
4. Shape dough into two logs along the length of the baking sheet, leaving room between them for spreading. Sprinkle with sea salt, if using.
5. Bake for 30 minutes, until golden and set. Remove from oven until cool enough to handle.
6. Cut into 1-inch slices, then place cut-side down onto baking sheet.
7. Return to oven; bake for 10 minutes, then flip and bake for 10 minutes on the second side.

Variation Add chocolate or caramel chips in addition to, or in place of, the nuts, to change up the flavor.

Plan Ahead Biscotti can be prepared ahead and frozen, well wrapped, until ready to use.

ENJOY

Honey Almond Oatmeal Blondies

Pareve | Yield 18 servings

I've written many times about the unexpected texture that oats give to baked goods, and these soft and delicious blondies are no different. They're bursting with honey flavor and have a great textural crunch, thanks to the almonds. If making these for Rosh Hashanah and you don't use almonds, feel free to skip them.

HONEY ALMOND CLUSTERS

- ¾ cup slivered almonds
- ¾ cup sliced almonds
- 2 Tablespoons brown sugar
- 2 Tablespoons honey
- 1 teaspoon cinnamon
- ½ teaspoon vanilla extract
- 1 Tablespoon oil

OATMEAL BLONDIES

- ¾ cup oil
- 2 eggs
- ½ cup brown sugar
- ¾ cup honey
- 1 teaspoon cinnamon
- 1 teaspoon vanilla extract
- ½ teaspoon sea salt
- 1 teaspoon baking soda
- 2 cups old-fashioned oats
- 1 cup flour

1. **Prepare the honey almond clusters:** Preheat oven to 400°F. Line a baking sheet with parchment paper. Set aside.
2. Place all honey almond clusters ingredients on prepared baking sheet. Toss to coat all nuts evenly; spread in a thin layer over baking sheet.
3. Bake for 10 minutes, stirring halfway through. Set aside to cool; then break apart to form small clusters.
4. **Prepare the oatmeal blondies:** Preheat oven to 350°F. Coat 2 (8-inch) pans with nonstick cooking spray.
5. In a medium bowl, whisk together oil, eggs, sugar, honey, cinnamon, vanilla, salt, and baking soda until smooth and creamy.
6. Add oats. Switch to a rubber spatula and mix until combined.
7. Add flour; stir until just combined. Mixture will be very thick. Stir in half of the almond mixture (see Note), then pour the batter into prepared pans.
8. Sprinkle remaining almond clusters over the batter in each pan. Bake for about 30 minutes, until the center is set. Cool in pan before slicing.

Note My testers were split on whether these were better with half of the nuts mixed in or all sprinkled on the top. If you like the textural contrast, mix in half. Otherwise, use to top batter before baking.

Plan Ahead Bars can be prepared and frozen until ready for use. For best results, freeze whole and cut before serving.

Strawberry Lemonade Bundt Cake

Dairy or Pareve | Yield 1 Bundt cake

There's something about strawberry lemonade that just makes me feel like it's a relaxed summer day — even if I'm sitting at my desk in the dead of the winter. This cake, with its bright and fresh lemon and strawberry flavors, has the same extraordinary properties of transforming even the gloomiest day to one full of fun summery memories.

- zest of 2 lemons
- 1½ cups sugar
- 5 eggs
- ½ cup oil
- 1 teaspoon baking soda
- 1 teaspoon baking powder
- 1 teaspoon vanilla extract
- ½ teaspoon sea salt
- ½ teaspoon lemon extract, optional but recommended
- 2½ cups flour
- ⅓ cup freshly squeezed lemon juice (from about 2 lemons)
- ⅔ cups milk OR nondairy milk
- ¾ cup chopped frozen strawberries tossed with 1 Tablespoon flour

LEMON GLAZE

- 1 cup powdered sugar
- 1 teaspoon lemon juice
- 1 Tablespoon corn syrup OR honey
- 1 Tablespoons hot water

1. Preheat oven to 350°F. Coat a Bundt pan with nonstick cooking spray and flour; set aside.
2. In a small bowl, mix lemon zest and sugar with a spoon to incorporate the lemon flavor. Add to bowl of electric mixer.
3. Add eggs and oil; beat on medium-high for a few minutes until combined and creamy.
4. Add baking soda, baking powder, vanilla, salt, and lemon extract. Beat until combined.
5. Turn mixer speed to low. Beating well after each addition, beat in half of the flour, followed by the lemon juice, followed by remaining flour, then the milk.
6. Pour ¾ of the batter into prepared Bundt pan. Top with strawberry/flour mixture, then add remaining batter.
7. Bake for about 45 minutes, until a toothpick inserted in the center comes out clean. Set cake aside to cool for 10 minutes, then invert and remove from pan. Transfer to a wire rack or platter. Cool completely before glazing.
8. **Prepare the lemon glaze:** Add all glaze ingredients to a small bowl; stir to combine. Drizzle over cooled cake.

Plan Ahead Cake can be prepared and frozen until ready to use. For best results, glaze just before serving.

Butterscotch Swirl Bundt Cake

Dairy or Pareve | Yield 1 Bundt cake

This is my original "viral" recipe, way back in 2012 when I first shared it. Every kosher grocery store sold out of butterscotch chips, and I got my first taste of what it meant that people all over the world were making and enjoying my recipes. It's still a favorite recipe, all these years later, and here it is, with some tweaks and adjustments to make it truly perfect.

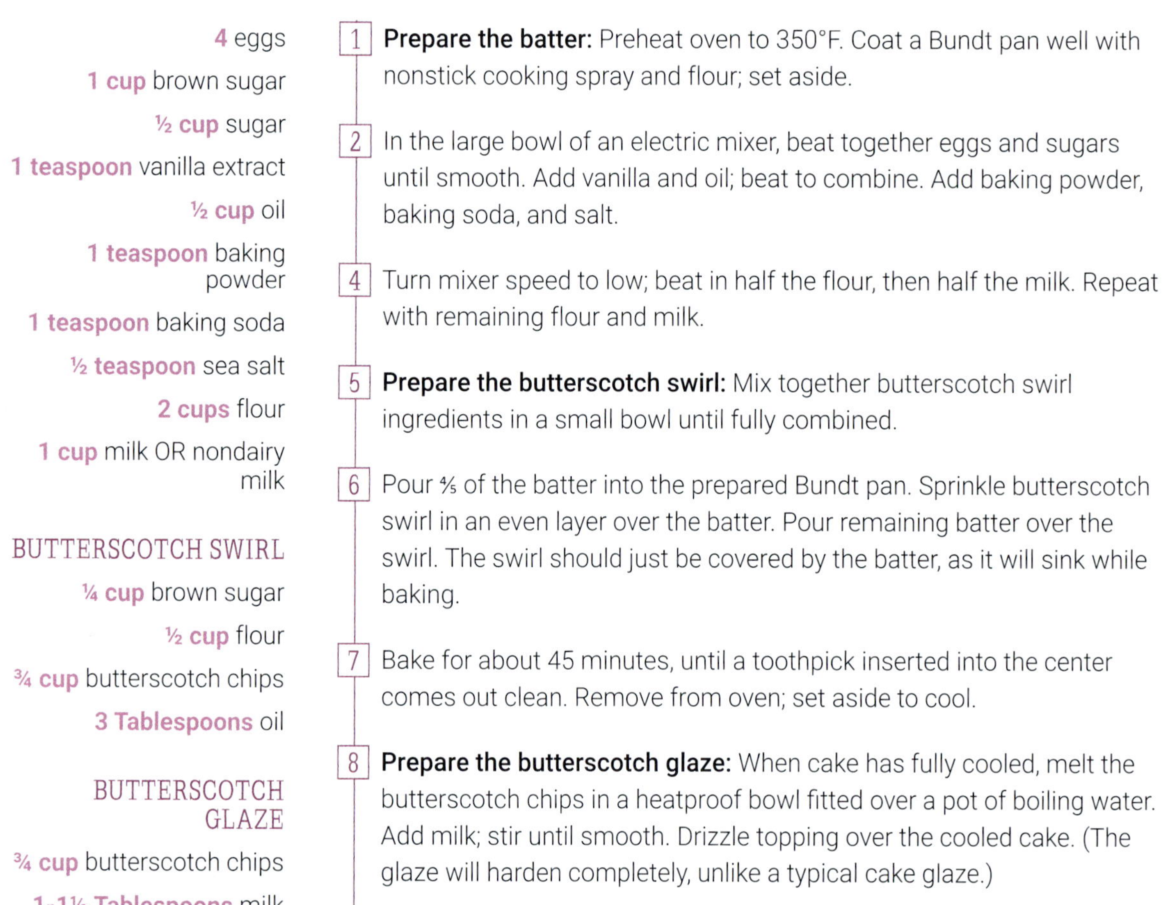

- **4** eggs
- **1 cup** brown sugar
- **½ cup** sugar
- **1 teaspoon** vanilla extract
- **½ cup** oil
- **1 teaspoon** baking powder
- **1 teaspoon** baking soda
- **½ teaspoon** sea salt
- **2 cups** flour
- **1 cup** milk OR nondairy milk

BUTTERSCOTCH SWIRL

- **¼ cup** brown sugar
- **½ cup** flour
- **¾ cup** butterscotch chips
- **3 Tablespoons** oil

BUTTERSCOTCH GLAZE

- **¾ cup** butterscotch chips
- **1-1½ Tablespoons** milk OR nondairy milk

1. **Prepare the batter:** Preheat oven to 350°F. Coat a Bundt pan well with nonstick cooking spray and flour; set aside.
2. In the large bowl of an electric mixer, beat together eggs and sugars until smooth. Add vanilla and oil; beat to combine. Add baking powder, baking soda, and salt.
4. Turn mixer speed to low; beat in half the flour, then half the milk. Repeat with remaining flour and milk.
5. **Prepare the butterscotch swirl:** Mix together butterscotch swirl ingredients in a small bowl until fully combined.
6. Pour ⅔ of the batter into the prepared Bundt pan. Sprinkle butterscotch swirl in an even layer over the batter. Pour remaining batter over the swirl. The swirl should just be covered by the batter, as it will sink while baking.
7. Bake for about 45 minutes, until a toothpick inserted into the center comes out clean. Remove from oven; set aside to cool.
8. **Prepare the butterscotch glaze:** When cake has fully cooled, melt the butterscotch chips in a heatproof bowl fitted over a pot of boiling water. Add milk; stir until smooth. Drizzle topping over the cooled cake. (The glaze will harden completely, unlike a typical cake glaze.)

Notes If you can't find butterscotch chips, you can use caramel chips instead. ■ If desired, sprinkle with sea salt flakes to garnish, as pictured.

Plan Ahead This cake freezes nicely when stored airtight. I wrap the cake in foil and then seal it in a ziplock bag. For best results, freeze it without the glaze, and add glaze just before serving.

Quadruple Chocolate Brownie Cake

Dairy or Pareve | Yield 1 (9x13-inch) cake

I have to admit, I wasn't expecting this cake at all when I first made it. I was trying to make something entirely different, but it was the best kind of surprise when this rich, brownie-like cake emerged from the oven, complete with the crackly brownie top!

CHOCOLATE CHIP STREUSEL

½ cup old-fashioned oats

½ cup flour

⅓ cup sugar

½ cup chocolate chips, preferably mini

¼ cup oil

BATTER

4 eggs

½ cup oil

2 cups sugar

1 (3.5-ounce) package instant chocolate pudding mix

1 teaspoon vanilla extract

1 teaspoon baking powder

1 teaspoon baking soda

pinch sea salt

⅔ cup cocoa powder

1½ cups flour

½ cup milk OR nondairy milk

½ cup chocolate liqueur

1. Preheat oven to 350°F. Coat a 9x13-inch baking pan well with nonstick cooking spray; set aside.
2. **Prepare the chocolate chip streusel:** In a small bowl, mix together all streusel ingredients to form a slightly damp mixture. Set aside.
3. **Prepare the batter:** In a large bowl or in the bowl of an electric mixer, whisk together eggs, oil, sugar, and pudding mix until combined.
4. Add vanilla, baking powder, baking soda, salt, and cocoa. Stir to combine.
5. Gradually stir in flour, then milk. Add chocolate liqueur. Mix until just combined.
6. Pour half the batter into prepared baking pan; top with chocolate chip streusel, followed by remaining batter.
7. Bake for about 55 minutes, until the top is set and crackly.

Plan Ahead This cake freezes nicely, well wrapped.

Cherry Cheesecake Crumb Cake

Dairy or Pareve | Yield Yield 2 (9-inch) cakes

This cake was inspired by a cherry cheesecake: cream cheese-infused batter, cherry pie filling dolloped over the top, and a graham cracker streusel topping. It's the kind of recipe you won't be able to resist … in the best possible way.

- 6 eggs
- 1 (8-ounces) bar cream cheese OR nondairy cream cheese
- 2 cups sugar
- 1 teaspoon baking powder
- juice of ½ lemon
- 1 teaspoon vanilla extract
- pinch sea salt
- 2½ cups flour
- 1 cup oil
- 1 (21-ounce) can cherry pie filling

CRUMB TOPPING

- 1 cup brown sugar
- 1 Tablespoon cinnamon
- 2½ cups graham cracker crumbs (see Note)
- ½ teaspoon sea salt
- 1 cup + 2 Tablespoons oil

1. Preheat oven to 325°F. Coat 2 (9-inch) round pans or springform pans with nonstick cooking spray; set aside.
2. In the bowl of an electric mixer fitted with the whisk attachment, beat together eggs and cream cheese until light in color, about 2 minutes.
3. Add sugar, baking powder, lemon juice, vanilla, and salt. Beat to combine. There may still be small pieces of cream cheese; this is normal.
4. Turn mixer speed to low. Beating to combine after each addition, add half the flour, followed by half of the oil, the remaining flour and the remaining oil. Divide mixture between prepared pans. Spoon cherry pie filling over the batter, distributing it evenly; set aside.
5. **Prepare the crumb topping:** Combine all topping ingredients in a medium bowl. Stir well to form a slightly damp mixture. Divide between pans to form a thick topping over the batter.
6. Bake for about 70 minutes, until top feels firm.

Note Don't process graham crackers until completely fine. Rather, leave a little texture, which results in a great crunch.

Variation Omit cherry pie filling to make a plain cheesecake crumb cake.

Plan Ahead Cake can be frozen, well wrapped, until ready to serve.

Stone Fruit Sticky Buns

Dairy or Pareve | Yield 2-2½ dozen buns

Biting into a juicy stone fruit is one of my favorite ways to enjoy summer produce. One day, I decided to try adding them to baked goods and haven't looked back. You're going to love the way the juicy fruits melt into the buns, creating the ultimate sticky-bottomed bun!

DOUGH

1 packet (2¼ teaspoons) dry active yeast

1 Tablespoon sugar

¼ cup warm water

¾ cup milk OR nondairy milk

⅓ cup oil

1 egg

2 egg yolks

1 teaspoon vanilla extract

¼ cup sugar

4 cups flour

ASSEMBLY

6 Tablespoons brown sugar

¾ cup oil

¾ cup sugar

2 teaspoons cinnamon

2 peaches, thinly sliced

2 nectarines, thinly sliced

2 plums, thinly sliced

1. **Prepare the dough:** Combine yeast, sugar, and water in the bowl of an electric mixer, fitted with the dough hook. Let mixture sit for about 5 minutes, until it starts to bubble.
2. Add remaining dough ingredients; beat until a smooth dough forms. Knead for about 5 minutes, until the dough is elastic and smooth.
3. Place dough in greased bowl; cover. Allow dough to rise in a warm space for about 2 hours, until doubled in bulk. Divide dough in half.
4. **Assemble the buns:** Preheat oven to 350°F. Coat 2 (9x13-inch) baking pans with nonstick cooking spray. Sprinkle 3 tablespoons brown sugar into each pan. Set aside.
5. In a small bowl, whisk together oil, sugar, and cinnamon; set aside.
6. On a floured surface, roll one piece of the dough as thin as you can, into a large rectangle. Spread half the oil and sugar mixture over it, then top with half of the fruit slices.
7. Carefully roll the dough into a log, rolling as tightly as you can. Cut the log into 1-inch slices; place slices into one of the prepared pans.
8. Repeat with remaining dough and fillings, dividing between pans.
9. Bake for 35-45 minutes, until the tops start to brown. These buns are best served warm.

Plan Ahead These buns can be frozen. For best results, reheat before serving.

Caramel Macchiato Rugelach

Pareve | Yield 4 dozen

Inspired by a perennial coffee shop favorite, this twist on a Jewish classic is bursting with bold flavors!

DOUGH

- **1 packet (2¼ teaspoons)** instant yeast
- **⅓ cup** warm water
- **½ cup** brown sugar
- **2** eggs
- **¾ cup** oil
- **pinch** sea salt
- **½ teaspoon** baking soda
- **2¾ cups** flour

FILLING

- **1 Tablespoon** instant coffee granules
- **3 Tablespoons** cocoa powder
- **3 Tablespoons** warm water
- **1 cup** brown sugar
- **½ teaspoon** cinnamon
- **1 teaspoon** vanilla extract
- **3 Tablespoons** oil

- **1** egg, lightly beaten, for brushing

OPTIONAL GLAZE

- **¾ cup** caramel chips
- **1-2 Tablespoons** nondairy milk

1. **Prepare the dough:** In the bowl of an electric mixer fitted with the dough hook, combine yeast and water; let sit for 2-3 minutes, until it starts to bubble. Add remaining dough ingredients; mix until a dough forms. Continue to knead for about 5 minutes, until dough is smooth. Place dough into a greased bowl; cover and set aside to rise for about 1 hour.
2. Preheat oven to 350°F. Line 2 baking sheets with parchment paper; set aside.
3. **Prepare the filling:** In a medium bowl, combine coffee, cocoa, and water to form a thick paste. Add brown sugar, cinnamon, vanilla, and oil; stir until smooth.
4. **Prepare the rugelach:** Divide dough into 3 pieces. Roll 1 portion of dough into a large round. Spread with ⅓ of the filling; cut the round into 16 wedges. Roll up each wedge, starting from the outer edge and ending at the point. Place on prepared baking sheet, point down. Repeat with remaining dough and filling. Brush beaten egg over the rugelach.
5. Bake for about 12 minutes, until golden brown.
6. **Prepared optional glaze:** In a small pot, melt together caramel chips and milk. Stir until smooth. Drizzle over cooled rugelach.

Plan Ahead These rugalach can be frozen in a sealed container or bag.

DAIRY-FREE BASIL PESTO, PAGE 292

HOMEMADE BOURBON BARBECUE SAUCE, PAGE 286

CEREAL CRUNCH CHOCOLATE CRUMBS, PAGE 294
CARAMEL CRUNCH CRUMBS, PAGE 294

HOMEMADE EVERYTHING BAGEL SPICE MIX, PAGE 290

CHOCOLATE GANACHE FOUR WAYS, PAGE 296

GUACAMOLE, PAGE 288
PICO DE GALLO, PAGE 288

Sauces *and* Staples

Homemade Bourbon Barbecue Sauce

Pareve | Yield about 4 cups

This sauce was going to be featured on the page with the Overnight Bourbon BBQ Ribs (page 156), but I decided that it's so good, and so delicious in a variety of recipes (try it in the BBQ Beef Lasagna, page 144), that it deserved a spotlight on its own!

1 Tablespoon oil
1 onion, diced
3 cloves garlic, minced
2 teaspoons kosher salt, divided
1 (6-ounce) can tomato paste
½ cup pure maple syrup
1 teaspoon hot sauce
1 Tablespoon soy sauce
1 teaspoon smoked paprika
¾ cup brown sugar
⅓ cup apple cider vinegar
¼ teaspoon ground ginger
¾ cup bourbon
½ cup ketchup
2 Tablespoons spicy brown mustard

1. Heat oil in a medium pot over medium-high heat. Add onion, garlic, and 1 teaspoon salt. Sauté for 5-8 minutes, until softened.
2. Add remaining ingredients; stir. Raise heat to high. Bring to a boil; reduce heat to low and simmer for 20-30 minutes, until thickened.
3. Use an immersion blender or food processor to blend the sauce until completely smooth.

Plan Ahead This sauce will stay fresh in the fridge in an airtight container for up to a week, or in the freezer for longer.

Guacamole

Pareve | Yield 3-4 cups

So many people buy guacomole at the grocery store. You'll be amazed at how easy it is to make and how much better it tastes!

- **3** avocados, peeled and pitted
- **2 cloves** garlic, minced
- juice of **1** lime
- **1** shallot OR **½** red onion, minced
- **1 teaspoon** kosher salt
- **½ teaspoon** cumin
- **pinch** cayenne pepper

1. Place avocados into a medium bowl. Use a fork, avocado masher, or potato masher to mash until smooth.
2. Add remaining ingredients; stir to combine.

Plan Ahead Guacamole can be made 1-2 days ahead and stored in an airtight container in the fridge.

Pico de Gallo

Parve | Yield about 3 cups

This is a quick and easy and tasty recipe that is made from vegetables that you often have in the kitchen. It makes a great fresh addition to any meal.

- **6** plum tomatoes, finely chopped
- **1 small** onion, very finely diced
- **3 cloves** garlic, minced
- **1** jalapeño pepper (use more or less to taste), very finely diced
- **3 Tablespoons** olive oil
- juice of **2** limes
- **1½ teaspoons** kosher salt
- **1 cup** fresh cilantro OR parsley, finely chopped

1. Place all ingredients into a large bowl; stir to combine.

Plan Ahead Pico de Gallo is best fresh but any leftovers can be served the next day.

Homemade Everything Bagel Spice Mix

Pareve | Yield about 1 cup

Everything bagel spice mix is so trendy lately — and people pay so much for little jars of it. The secret is that it's so easy to make your own, so make a big batch and keep it around for everything from grilled chicken to topping a sunny-side-up egg, to the traditional use of topping your homemade challahs and bread.

- **3 Tablespoons** dried minced onion
- **3 Tablespoons** dried minced garlic
- **2 Tablespoons** poppy seeds
- **2 Tablespoons** black sesame seeds
- **2 Tablespoons** white sesame seeds
- **1 Tablespoon** coarse or flake salt

1. Place all ingredients into a small bowl. Stir to combine.
2. Heat a frying pan over high heat. Add mixture to dry pan; pan fry, stirring almost constantly, for 2-3 minutes, until mixture starts to brown a little.
3. Remove from heat; allow to cool before using.

Plan Ahead Spice mix can be stored at room temperature in an airtight container for 2-3 weeks.

Dairy-Free Basil Pesto

Pareve | Yield about 3 cups

Traditionally, pesto gets a boost of flavor from Parmesan cheese, but to keep this dairy-free, I use fresh lemon to take it to the next level!

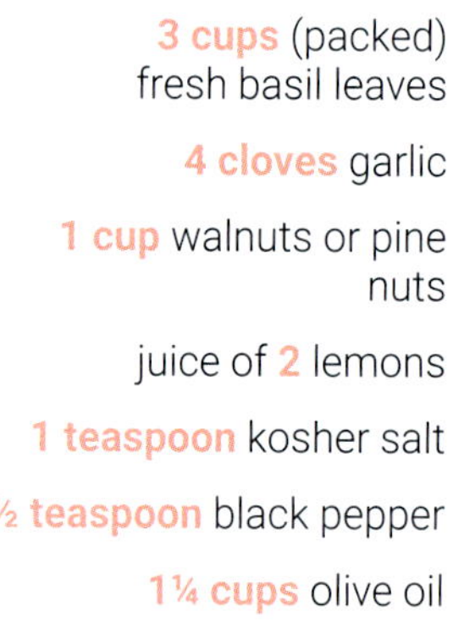

3 cups (packed) fresh basil leaves

4 cloves garlic

1 cup walnuts or pine nuts

juice of 2 lemons

1 teaspoon kosher salt

½ teaspoon black pepper

1¼ cups olive oil

1. Place basil, garlic, nuts, lemon juice, salt, and pepper in the bowl of a blender.

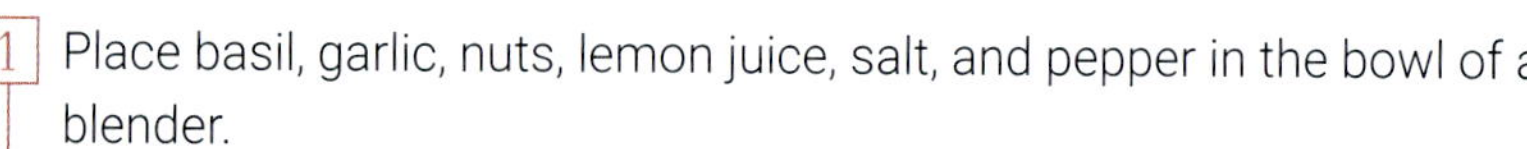

2. With the blender running, slowly add oil; blend well until fully combined.

Plan Ahead Pesto can be stored in the fridge for about a week. It can be frozen (I like to freeze it in 1-2-tablespoon portions in an ice cube tray) for longer.

Cereal Crunch Chocolate Crumbs

Pareve | Yield about 4 cups

Caramel Crunch Crumbs

Pareve | Yield 2 cups

Easy to prepare and so versatile, both of these crunchy and satisfying crumb recipes are great for so many uses, such as on Chocolate Mousse (page 230), on top of ice cream, or mixed into your yogurt for a breakfast treat!

Cereal Crunch Chocolate Crumbs

3 cups chocolate cereal, crushed (see Note)

1 cup flour

¾ cup cocoa powder

¾ cup sugar

1 teaspoon baking powder

pinch kosher salt

1 egg, lightly beaten

½ cup oil

1. Preheat oven to 375°F. Line a baking sheet with parchment paper; set aside.
2. In a medium bowl, mix together cereal, flour, cocoa, sugar, baking powder, and salt until combined.
3. Add egg and oil; mix until coarse, uneven crumbs form.
4. Spread mixture on prepared baking sheet. Bake for about 8-10 minutes, until somewhat crispy.

Notes Cereal should be crushed by hand, to ensure that some texture remains in the final crumbs. ■ Use your favorite chocolate-flavored cereal here; my personal preference is Oreo O's.

Plan Ahead Both types of crumbs can be stored in a ziplock bag in the freezer until ready to use.

Caramel Crunch Crumbs

9 whole graham crackers (1 sleeve)

1 cup old-fashioned oats

1 teaspoon vanilla extract

¼ cup canola oil

¾ cup caramel OR butterscotch chips

1. Preheat oven to 350°F; line a baking sheet with parchment paper. Set aside.
2. Place the graham crackers into a medium bowl and crush using a heavy utensil such as a wooden rolling pin. Crush into crumbs and some slightly larger pieces — you want to retain some texture.
3. Add oats, vanilla, and oil to the bowl; stir to combine so that the crumbs are slightly wet. Spread the crumb mixture over the prepared cookie sheet.
4. Bake the crumbs for 8 minutes. Remove from oven and immediately stir in the caramel chips. The heat of the hot crumbs will help melt the chips and distribute the flavor.
5. Set aside to cool completely.

Chocolate Ganache Four Ways

Dairy or Pareve | Yield about 3 cups

Chocolate ganache is one of the easiest — and most versatile — chocolate recipes. Not only does it require only a small number of ingredients, but it comes together in minutes. When hot, it's a liquid that you can drizzle over your ice cream or use to garnish your dessert. When room temperature or cold, it's solid enough to form into balls: the perfect truffle filling. Just roll the balls in cocoa or cookie crumbs or dip into melted chocolate for a rich and delightful candy.

1. Place a heatproof bowl over a small pot of boiling water over low heat.
2. Add desired flavor ingredients to bowl; heat, stirring occasionally, until chocolate is melted and mixture is smooth.

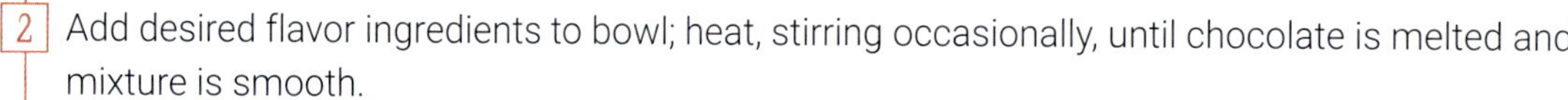

TRADITIONAL

8 ounces semi-sweet chocolate, chopped

½ cup heavy whipping cream OR nondairy whip, unwhipped

1 teaspoon vanilla extract

PEANUT BUTTER

8 ounces semi-sweet chocolate, chopped

⅓ cup heavy whipping cream OR nondairy whip, unwhipped

⅓ cup creamy peanut butter

STRAWBERRY

8 ounces semi-sweet chocolate, chopped

¼ cup heavy whipping cream OR nondairy whip, unwhipped

¼ cup strawberry jam

MOCHA

8 ounces semi-sweet chocolate, chopped

¼ cup heavy whipping cream OR nondairy whip, unwhipped

1 Tablespoon instant coffee granules dissolved in **¼ cup** boiling water

Plan Ahead Chocolate ganache will keep for a week or two in the fridge. If you plan to serve it warm and liquidy, make sure to rewarm over gentle heat, as when it was originally made.

Pesach Guide

Adjust recipes as indicated in parentheses for use on Pesach.

Index

D

S

T

V

W

Z